CULTURES OF THE WORLD

# LUXEMBOURG

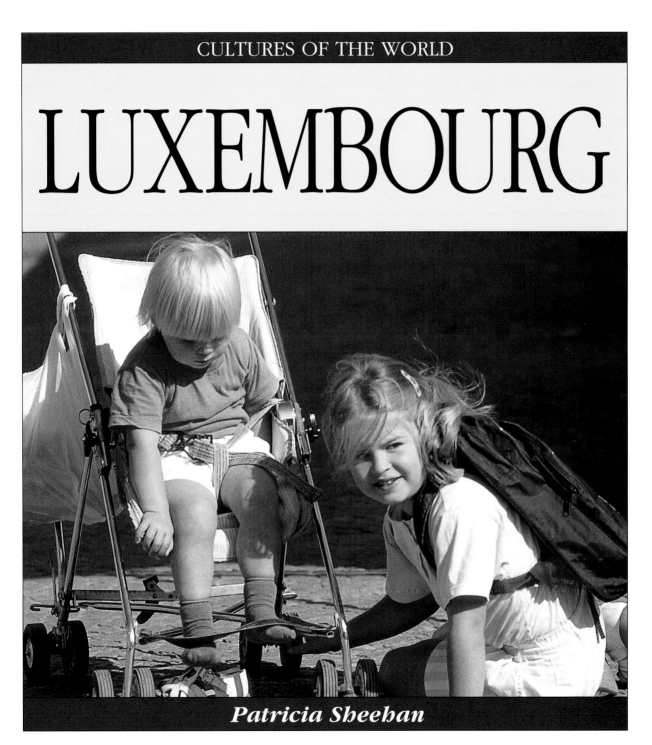

*Patricia Sheehan*

MARSHALL CAVENDISH
*New York • London • Sydney*

Reference Edition published 1999 by
Marshall Cavendish Corporation
99 White Plains Road
Tarrytown
New York 10591

© Times Editions Pte Ltd 1997

Originated and designed by
Times Books International, an imprint of
Times Editions Pte Ltd

Printed in Malaysia

*Library of Congress Cataloging-in-Publication Data:*
Sheehan, Patricia.
    Luxembourg / Patricia Sheehan.
        p. cm.—(Cultures Of The World)
    Includes bibliographical references and index.
    Summary: Discusses the geography, history, government,
economy, and customs of the smallest of the Benelux countries.
    ISBN 0-7614-0685-9 (library binding)
    1. Luxembourg—Juvenile literature. [1. Luxembourg.]
I. Title. II. Series.
DH905.954 1997
914.935—dc21            96–53367
                    CIP
                    AC

# INTRODUCTION

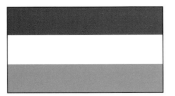

Luxembourg, often called the Grand Duchy, is not only one of the smallest nations in Western Europe; it is also among the richest, with a thriving banking and financial industry, and successes on other economic fronts. Strategically located between France, Germany, and Belgium, the country has been a battleground throughout much of its history, with frequent invasions by various foreign powers. Nonetheless, Luxembourg has managed to carve out its place as an independent nation with its own unique culture.

Today the Grand Duchy is the cradle of modern Europe, thanks to its pivotal role in the development of the European Community, the forerunner of the European Union (EU), and is home to many of the EU's prestigious institutions, including the European Court of Justice and the European Investment Bank. With so many different nationalities working and living within its borders, Luxembourg has become one of the continent's most cosmopolitan countries.

# CONTENTS

Castle ruins near the town of Diekirch offer a reminder of Luxembourg's rich past.

**3**  INTRODUCTION

**7**  GEOGRAPHY
*Green heart of Europe • Rivers and lakes • Climate • Flora and fauna • Major cities*

**19**  HISTORY
*Celtic and Roman rule • A medieval world • Foreign domination • Moves towards national independence • Wars and occupation • Modern Luxembourg • The European Union*

**29**  GOVERNMENT
*Constitutional rights • Representation of the people • Public administration • Local government • Law of the land • The royal family • The political divide • Women in politics*

**37**  ECONOMY
*A success story • Workforce • Social consensus • An eye for opportunities • Industry • Trade fairs • Financial services • Agriculture • Tourism • Exports and imports*

**49**  LUXEMBOURGERS
*Population trends • National pride • Character and personality • Melting pot • Dress • Prominent Luxembourgers*

**57**  LIFESTYLE
*Standard of living • Hearth and home • Family values • Women • Young people • Education • The welfare state • Crime and punishment • Green living • Environmental planning*

**69**  RELIGION
*From Druids to Christianity • A medieval center • The Protestant challenge • Witchcraft • Religion today • Places of worship*

# CONTENTS

**77** LANGUAGE
*Rivalry of languages • Three languages, three uses • Luxembourgish in the arts • Standardizing Luxembourgish • Learning Luxembourgish • Popular names • Broadcasting and newspapers*

**87** ARTS
*Archaeology • Traditional crafts • Theater and cinema • Music • Painting and sculpture • Cultural monuments and architecture • Modern architecture*

**97** LEISURE
*Vacations • National sports • Recreation • Entertainment*

**103** FESTIVALS
*National Day • Easter • Christmas • New Year • Customs and rituals • Fairs and fetes • Religious festivals*

**113** FOOD
*Traditional fare • Eating habits • Specialties • A nation of drinkers • Wines • Seasonal foods • Eating out*

**122** MAP OF LUXEMBOURG

**124** QUICK NOTES

**125** GLOSSARY

**126** BIBLIOGRAPHY

**126** INDEX

A drive along the Moselle provides some of the most scenic views of the country.

# GEOGRAPHY

LUXEMBOURG IS ONE OF THE NATIONS, along with Belgium and the Netherlands, collectively known as the Benelux countries. This name arose from trading partnerships established after World War II.

Luxembourg is smaller than the state of Rhode Island. It measures 55 miles (80 km) long and 35 miles (55 km) wide, covering some 998 square miles (2,586 square km). Triangular in shape and bordering Belgium in the west, Germany in the east, and France in the south, with 221 miles (356 km) of borders, the country is completely landlocked.

Despite its small size, Luxembourg has a varied topography, with two main features to the landscape. The northern section of the country is formed by part of the plateau of the Ardennes, where the mountains range from 1,500 to almost 2,000 feet (460–610 m) high. The rest of the country is made up of undulating countryside with broad valleys. The capital, Luxembourg City, is located in the southern part of the country.

*Opposite:* **Vineyards line the deep valleys flanking the Moselle, which separates the lower eastern half of Luxembourg from its large neighbor, Germany.**

*Left:* **The road to Belgium. The Benelux countries are also referred to as the Low Countries—this from Roman times when these low-lying lands around the mouth of the Rhine River and its subsidiaries were the vital door to much of the continent.**

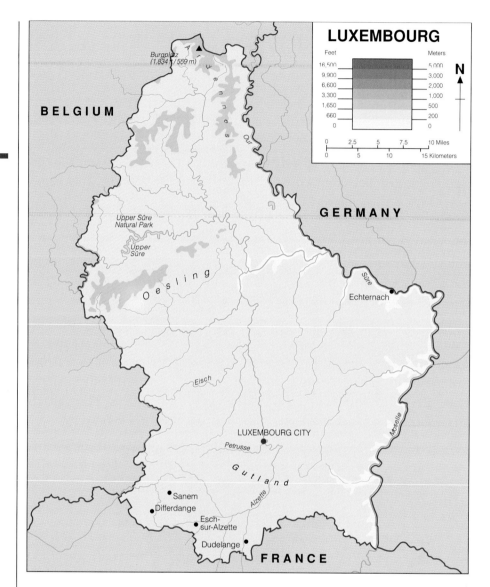

## GREEN HEART OF EUROPE

The most prominent landmark, the high plateau of the Ardennes in the north, took nature millions of years to carve. At its highest point, it reaches a height of 1,834 feet (559 m). Commonly known as the Oesling, the Ardennes region covers 325 square miles (842 square km), about 32% of the entire country.

Rugged scenery predominates because river erosion over thousands of years has left a varied, low mountain landscape, densely covered with vegetation, sometimes with considerable variations in height. These differences in relief, together with stretches of water interspersed with forests, fields, and pastures, are the main features that make the landscape so distinctive. Typical of this high area, however, is infertile soil and poor drainage resulting in numerous peat bogs, which were once exploited as fuel. These factors, combined with heavy rainfall and frost, made this an inhospitable environment for the first settlers.

Even today, the living conditions in such an environment are not particularly favorable. Nevertheless, some 7,800 people make a living off the land, either through forestry, small-scale farming, or environmental work. Because the soil is so difficult to cultivate, most of the land is used for cattle pasture. The Ardennes region also includes the Upper Sûre Natural Park, an important conservation area and a hikers' retreat.

South of the Sûre River the country is known as the Gutland. This region covers slightly over two-thirds of the country.

Beef cattle are raised on the rich pastures of the hill slopes near the town of Vianden in the north-eastern part of the country.

Luxembourg's vineyards produce wines that are especially appreciated in Belgium, with some 80% of exports going to this neighbor.

The terrain gently rises and falls with an average height of 700 ft (213 m). Agriculture is the main activity as the term Gutland arises from the fertile soils and warm, dry summers experienced in this part of the Duchy compared to the Oesling region.

As a result, vegetables and fruit, such as strawberries, apples, plums, and cherries, are grown in large quantities. River erosion in this area has created deep gorges and caves resulting in some spectacular scenery.

In the extreme south of the country lies "the land of the red rocks"— a reference to the deposits of minerals found here. Rich in iron ore since Roman, if not earlier, times, the district is a mining and heavy industrial region that stretches for over 12.4 miles (20 km). The tall chimneys of the iron and steel works are typical landmarks of the industrial south.

To the east lies the grape-growing valley of the Moselle. Numerous villages nestle in the deep valleys and behind the vineyards along the river banks. Every village has at least one winery. Also in the east is the "Little Switzerland" area, characterized by wooded glens and ravines with unusual rock formations.

## RIVERS AND LAKES

Luxembourg has a number of minor rivers, such as the Eisch, the Alzette, and the Petrusse, but the main river is the Moselle with its tributaries—the Sûre and the Our. Together, their courses serve as a natural boundary between Luxembourg and Germany. Along their banks, many of the country's medieval castles can be found.

The Moselle River actually rises in northeast France and flows north through Luxembourg for 19 miles (30.6 km) to join the mighty Rhine at Koblenz, Germany. The Moselle is 320 miles (514 km) long, and is navigable, due to canalization, for 40 miles (64 km). Green slopes, covered with vines, flank the meandering course of the river.

Rising in Belgium, the Sûre River flows for 107 miles (172 km) in an easterly direction through Luxembourg and into the Moselle. Its sinuous course essentially cuts Luxembourg from east to west. The Our River, flowing along the northeastern border, is a tributary of the Sûre. Its valley is surrounded by unspoiled countryside.

The Moselle River, which has its source in the Vosges Mountains of France, eventually flows into the Rhine in Germany.

*The main principle underlying ecosystem protection in the Upper Sûre Natural Park is that the environment is an integral network in which each element interacts and affects the functioning of the whole.*

The Upper Sûre lake is the largest stretch of water in the Grand Duchy. Surrounded by luxuriant vegetation and peaceful creeks, the lake is a center for water sports, such as sailing, canoeing, and kayaking. Such outdoor activities, which make it an attractive spot for visitors, has led to the growth of a local crafts industry.

The town of Esch-sur-Sûre nestles at one end of the lake. Immediately above it, the river has been dammed to form a hydroelectric reservoir extending some 6 miles (10 km) up the valley. The Upper Sûre dam was built in the sixties to meet the country's drinking water requirements.

## THE UPPER SÛRE NATURAL PARK

Located in the far northwest of the Oesling area, the Natural Park is primarily an area of conservation and a specially protected area for wild birds. The objectives of the park are threefold.

First, and most importantly, the aim is to protect the natural environment and ecosystem. This means preserving the indigenous flora and fauna as well as protecting the purity of air, water, and soil quality. A second goal is to develop economic activity, mostly forestry and low-density tourism, as a means of creating employment and a high quality of life. As a result, the transportation infrastructure throughout the park is excellent.

For visitors to the park, there is a host of leisure activities, from nature walks, to tours of cultural monuments, to water sports on the Upper Sûre lake. More than 310 miles (500 km) of well-maintained footpaths make this a popular spot for day trippers with a wide range of accommodation for the vacationer. A fair and festival is held in the park annually on the first weekend in July.

The third objective is to preserve the architectural heritage of the area, which ranges from large numbers of chapels and disused mills to former slate quarries and castle ruins.

*Opposite:* **Wine experts believe it is the spring and summer weather that determines the quality of wine that is produced.**

## CLIMATE

Luxembourg is part of the West European Continental climatic region, and enjoys a temperate climate without extremes. Winters are mild, summers fairly cool, and rainfall is high.

Seasonal weather is somewhat different between the northern and southern regions. In the north there is considerable influence from the Atlantic systems, in which the passage of frequent pressure depressions gives rise to unstable weather conditions. This results in changeable weather with constant overcast skies and considerable drizzle in the winter.

Rainfall reaches 49 inches (1.2 m) a year in some areas. In the summer, excessive heat is rare and temperatures drop noticeably at night. Low temperatures and humidity make for what those living in this part of the country call, optimistically, an "invigorating climate."

In the south, although the rainfall is not significantly lower, at around 32 inches (80 cm), and the winters no milder, the principal difference is in the higher summer temperatures, especially in the Moselle valley. Crops, especially wine grapes, thrive here. With a mean annual temperature of 10°C (50°F), the sunniest months are May to August. In spring, the countryside is a riot of wildflowers and blossoms.

A field of red poppies in full bloom in the countryside.

## *FLORA AND FAUNA*

Luxembourg's flora is characterized by the country's location at the border between the Atlantic-European and Central European vegetation zones. In the north, beech and oak trees are plentiful. The oak trees can grow up to 100–150 feet (30–45 m) high, with a diameter of 4–8 feet (1.2–2.4 m). They supply large quantities of excellent hardwood timber because of their strength.

Along the riverbanks, species like the black alder and willow can be found. Alder wood is pale yellow to reddish brown, fine-textured and durable even under water. It is also an important timber tree mainly because of its disease-resistant properties. Willow trees can reach a height of 65 feet (20 m) and are valued for ornamental purposes.

The narrow, deeply incised valleys of the north also provide a habitat for rare plants and animals, especially the otter, a protected species. In the industrial south, among the abandoned quarries and deserted open pit mines, nature has reclaimed her own, and there are flowers everywhere.

### THE OTTER

The otter has a slender body, weighing 13–33 lbs (6–15 kg), a long neck, small ears, and short legs. The base of its tail is almost as thick as its body. With its webbed feet, it is an accomplished swimmer, and can travel underwater for quarter of a mile (0.4 km) without surfacing for air. Even on land, the otter can travel faster than a human can run.

It eats small aquatic animals, but also preys on small mammals. The otter is a playful animal, with a favorite pastime of sliding down steep banks of mud or snow and plunging into water or snowdrifts.

## *MAJOR CITIES*

With Luxembourg's small population, the only true city is the capital itself. The usual settlement in Luxembourg is a small town, with the majority of people choosing this type of urban living rather than residing in rural parts of the country.

**Luxembourg City** The capital occupies a dramatic and picturesque site on a high point above precipitous cliffs that drop to the narrow valleys of the Alzette and Petrusse rivers. The 230-foot (70-m) deep gorge cut by the Alzette, spanned by bridges and viaducts, adds to the charm of the city. Although the original fortress over which Luxembourg City is built was demolished in 1867, some of the defensive fortifications remain intact. As a result, there are superb viewpoints over the city and the opportunity to visit the casemates hewn into the rock.

Though Luxembourg City is not large, its layout is complex, as the city is set on several levels.

Luxembourg City is a cosmopolitan European capital with much in the way of evening entertainment, especially in the warmer months.

Despite progressive urbanization, the capital still retains a certain tranquillity. There are numerous shops selling international goods, bistros, and restaurants with numerous specialties from all over the world. The combination of multilingual cultural events, the central location, space for offices and businesses, as well as excellent transport links, make Luxembourg a capital city of renown in Europe. It has a population of some 76,000.

**Esch-sur-Alzette** This is the second largest town in the country and the principal one in the industrial south. Located near the French border, the town is an ancient settlement that can be traced back to more than 5,000 years ago. Its name is derived from the Celtic word *esk,* meaning a stream. Esch-sur-Alzette has an established reputation, both as a business center and as an architectural town due to its art-deco houses.

The cosmopolitan town, with a large number of foreign residents, also has numerous entertainment and cultural attractions. About four miles (six

km) outside the town is a museum displaying mining activities in the 19th and 20th centuries. The site of the famous French grotto of Our Lady of Lourdes is very close to the town. Some 24,000 people live in Esch-sur-Alzette.

**Differdange**, **Dudelange**, and **Sanem**, with populations of 15,700, 14,700, and 11,500 respectively, are all industrial towns with economies based on the iron and steel industries. They each have commercial centers, with pleasant parks and recreational sites.

**Echternach** This town lies on the banks of the Sûre, which forms the border with Germany. The town is especially well-known for the dancing procession that takes place each Whit Tuesday. The old patrician houses, narrow streets, Benedictine Abbey, and ancient walls have helped Echternach to retain a remarkable medieval atmosphere.

The town square in Echternach. The town was once one of the most important religious centers of Europe. It was here that the art of medieval manuscript illumination developed and reached its height during the 11th century. Today, it has a population of some 4,000.

# HISTORY

THE RICH HISTORY OF LUXEMBOURG explains how one of the smallest independent states in the world came into existence and how a population the size of an average European city has developed an unmistakable culture, language, and identity.

Luxembourg was once a larger country, owning large areas of what is now Belgium, France, and Germany, but foreign domination and rule reduced the territory of Luxembourg considerably.

## *CELTIC AND ROMAN RULE*

The Celts, early inhabitants of Luxembourg, were an Iron Age people, able to make more sophisticated weapons than their predecessors, who only used stone and bone for tools. They were a strong race of warriors who drove chariots and faced one another in single combat. But despite their strength and resistance, they were no competition for Julius Caesar, who arrived in 58 B.C. and conquered all the land up to the Rhine.

By 15 B.C., Luxembourg, along with the other two Low Countries, Belgium and the Netherlands, had become an imperial province of the Roman Empire under Emperor Augustus. Roman rule continued until the middle of the fifth century, when the Germanic Franks occupied most of the country. By the eighth century, Frankish King Charlemagne had been declared emperor by the pope.

For the next 200 years, until the 10th century, the former imperial province was the subject of continuous fighting by competing counts, lords, and dukes.

*Above:* **Julius Caesar overran Gaul and the surrounding region, including Luxembourg, in a series of military campaigns between 58 and 50 B.C.**

*Opposite:* **William II (ruled 1840–1849) is the Duchy's most respected Dutch ruler.**

19

**Vianden Castle, one of the many medieval forts found around the country.**

---

*At the peak of its political power in the 14th and 15th centuries, Luxembourg provided four rulers who served as Holy Roman Emperors.*

## A MEDIEVAL WORLD

Between the 10th and 14th centuries, the County of Luxembourg began to take shape. A tower had been built many years earlier on an important crossroad, forming part of the Roman defense system against Germanic tribes. Known as the *Castellum Lucilinburhuc* ("CA-stel-um LUK-in-burr-huk"), or "Little Castle," this stronghold became the property of Siegfried, Count of the Ardennes, in 963.

He immediately began to build a fortified castle on a neighboring rock known as the "Bock," at the junction of two rivers, the Alzette and the Petrusse. This castle became the foundation of the city of Luxembourg, and over the course of time, strong circular walls were built for its defense.

Luxembourg was able to remain independent until the 14th century mainly because of several strong personalities who emerged during this period. One of the most important was Countess Ermesinde, who in the 13th century, ruled for over 20 years. During her reign, Ermesinde extended considerably the frontiers of Luxembourg, not by war, but through the peaceful means of marriage alliances. In those times, marriages were more powerful than wars in terms of allegiance and loyalty.

Another powerful figure was the 14th-century Count John the Blind. By the age of 41, he had completely lost his sight. Nonetheless, he managed to increase Luxembourg's holdings, stimulate the economy, set up a new defense system, and build new fortifications. John typified the medieval knight for whom honor, loyalty, and courage were key qualities. He remains a national hero to Luxembourgers today.

Under the rule of his son Charles, Luxembourg reached its greatest expanse, through treaties and his own and family marriages. In 1354, Luxembourg's status was raised from that of a county to a duchy.

## ERMESINDE—THE FOUNDING LADY OF LUXEMBOURG

Ermesinde, born as the only heir when her father was 40 years old, was betrothed from birth to one of the most powerful princes in the Kingdom of France, the Count of Champagne. However, he married the Queen of Jerusalem instead, and so Ermesinde, at the tender age of 12, was "passed" to a cousin, Count Theobald. During the life of Theobald, then already in his forties and a grandfather from a first marriage, Ermesinde took little part in political affairs.

On Theobold's death in 1214, she was a young woman of 27 years and a desirable match, with four daughters but no male heir. At the beginning of the 13th century, succession through the female line was not ensured, and so to protect her inheritance she married a German prince with whom she had a son, Henry V.

Upon the death of her second husband in 1226, Ermesinde began a personal reign—which lasted 20 years, a considerable length of rule in medieval times—until her son came of age. During this period, she established the foundations of the Luxembourg state, granted a charter to the City of Luxembourg, and proved to be a political woman of great maturity. Under her rule, the citizens of Luxembourg gained much personal freedom, including the right to sell possessions, organize themselves, and create institutions. Ermesinde became known as the Founding Lady of Luxembourg.

*Before the 14th century, there had been little outside interest in the Low Countries but when thriving fishing, shipping, and textile industries developed, foreign rulers were quick to move in.*

**Napoleon Bonaparte (1769–1821)—emperor of France from 1804 to 1815.**

## *FOREIGN DOMINATION*

From the 15th to the 18th centuries, Luxembourg and the other Low Countries fell under a succession of foreign rulers—the French Burgundians, the Austrian Habsburgs, the Spanish, and then the French again. By 1506, with the King of Spain in power, the Netherlands had became disillusioned with Catholicism and Spanish rule. They rebelled in 1566 and declared their independence. Luxembourg and Belgium remained Catholic and under Spanish control, with a brief return to Austrian rule, until the French invasion by Napoleon Bonaparte in 1795. Through annexation, much of Luxembourg's territory became part of France.

## *MOVES TOWARD NATIONAL INDEPENDENCE*

The modern Luxembourg state has its origins in the Treaty of Vienna in 1815, which attempted to reorganize Europe after the defeat of Napoleon Bonaparte. The Duchy was raised to the rank of a Grand Duchy and became part of the Kingdom of the Netherlands, along with the Netherlands and Belgium.

By 1839, Belgium had established itself as an independent kingdom, and Luxembourg was partitioned, losing much of its territory to the new Belgian state. It was not until 1867 in the Treaty of London that Luxembourg, greatly reduced in size, was formally recognized as independent and guaranteed permanent neutrality.

A union with the Netherlands ended in 1890 when King William III of the Netherlands died, and Wilhelmina became Queen of the Netherlands. Luxembourg refused to recognize Wilhelmina as monarch because there was a male heir, Duke Adolphe, in a branch of the House of Luxembourg.

## GIBRALTAR OF THE NORTH

Over a period of 400 years, the fortress of Luxembourg was besieged, devastated, and rebuilt more than 20 times. In 1795, French General Carnot described the city as "second only to Gibraltar," a reference to the famous Rock of Gibraltar in Spain, which too was continually stormed, but rarely captured. A compliment indeed to the impregnability of Luxembourg's fortress.

Under the Treaty of London in 1867 that granted independence to Luxembourg, it was agreed that the old fortress, considered a symbol of war and devastation, was to be destroyed. By this time, after nine centuries of military architecture, the fortress had, for its defense, three battlements built with 24 forts: the first was fortified with bastions, the second included 15 forts, and the third was composed of an exterior wall counting nine forts. With an additional 47,840 sq yards (40,000 sq meters) of military barracks, the dismantling took 16 years to complete.

It is possible today to walk along the imposing remains of one of the most powerful fortresses in Europe. Some 7 miles (11 km) of the former 15 miles (24 km) of underground defenses called casemates (basically tunnels cut deep into the rock to give besieged troops shelter) still exist. It was impossible to destroy the casemates without also destroying the city, so only the main connections and entrances were closed. Some of the casemates have several floors connected by huge staircases descending more than 120 feet (36.6 m). Used as bomb shelters during the World Wars, they also doubled up as nuclear shelters during the Cold War.

# WARS AND OCCUPATION

During World War I, despite its neutrality, Luxembourg was occupied by German troops. After the war ended, all previous economic ties with Germany were severed, and the Grand Duchy joined Belgium in an economic union in 1921. Until the outbreak of World War II, the Grand Duchy, under the reign of Grand Duchess Charlotte, made good economic progress.

In May 1940, German troops invaded Luxembourg and the Duchess was forced to flee. She established a government-in-exile in England. Thousands of young men were pressed into the German armies by the Nazi occupiers, although a strong Resistance movement was organized. After five years of occupation Luxembourg was finally liberated by allied forces under American General George S. Patton's command in April 1945.

## BATTLE OF THE BULGE

With allied successes on all fronts, it appeared that Germany would be defeated by Christmas 1944. But attention focused sharply on Luxembourg on December 16, 1944, when it became clear that the Germans had started a major offensive through the northern part of its territory.

General Patton had envisioned a German surprise attack and as a result had three contingency plans drawn up. He transmitted one of these to his army and the entire force made a 90 degree turn towards the north, pushing through Luxembourg. They hit the advancing German units in the flanks on the southern shoulder of the "Bulge," a term used to describe the layout of the land. During fierce combat that took place under adverse winter conditions, Patton's army defeated the enemy by the end of January. The Battle of the Bulge took out Nazi Germany's last operational reserves and, by May 1945, they had unconditionally surrendered.

Despite this resounding success, President Harry Truman relieved Patton of his command in October 1945 because of the General's fierce antagonism toward communism. Convinced that his destiny lay in military glory, Patton was accused of being arrogant and vain, which, unfortunately, earned him many enemies. Many saw him, however, as a true Southern gentleman, prizing bravery above all other virtues. He remains a national hero to Luxembourgers. Patton is buried in the Hamm US military cemetery in Luxembourg, amongst the men from the Third Army that he commanded.

## THE LUXEMBOURG RESISTANCE

Barraged by Nazi propaganda during World War II, the Luxembourg Resistance organized counter-propaganda, such as secret newspapers, photos, and badges. These carried either the picture of Grand Duchess Charlotte or the national colors to keep up morale.

The Resistance's most important contribution was the passing on of vital information to the Allies, which influenced the course of the war and caused considerable damage to the Nazis. Penalties for such activities were severe, but this did not deter the Resistance movement.

Not far from the border with Poland, at Peenemunde, the Germans had set up a research center for the development of a long range rocket. The secret base, though well-guarded, needed a large workforce to run it, which was supplied by prisoners of war. A number of young Luxembourgers were forced to work on the base and quickly realized what was going on. An ingenious method of getting out the information to avoid censorship was conceived, and the network was never discovered or the people involved caught. Unfortunately, some of these brave Luxembourgers died on their way home to Luxembourg at the end of the war.

## *MODERN LUXEMBOURG*

The Grand Duchess Charlotte reigned for 45 years from 1919 to 1964, a period, except for the interruptions of the World Wars, of general prosperity for Luxembourgers. The present Grand Duke Jean succeeded to the throne after the abdication of his mother. The Duke is married to Princess Josephine-Charlotte of Belgium.

In 1948, after the deprivation of World War II, Luxembourg gave up its neutrality by joining various international organizations. These included the United Nations (UN), the North Atlantic Treaty Organization (NATO), and the Organization for Economic Cooperation and Development (OECD). Through these organizations, and the Benelux Customs Union in 1947 with Belgium and Netherlands, Luxembourg has supported a policy of cooperation on the international front, and in the post-war period, enjoyed unprecedented peace and economic prosperity.

**Grand Duke Jean and Princess Josephine-Charlotte after their marriage ceremony in 1953.**

In 1951, Luxembourg, the other Benelux countries, plus Germany, France, and Italy decided to form the six-member European Coal and Steel Community (ECSC). Playing a major role in this plan was Luxembourg born-and-raised French Foreign Minister Robert Schuman.

Based on the understanding that if an individual nation did not control its heavy industries or key industries for armaments, then it could no longer declare war, this became the first step to European integration.

## THE EUROPEAN UNION

The second stage of European unification came soon after, in 1958, with the establishment of the European Economic Community (EEC), an institution set up to facilitate free trade of goods and services among the six member countries. By 1990, membership had increased to 12. The Maastricht Treaty, the third stage, led to the creation of the European Union (EU) in 1993 and set the scene for the even more ambitious goal of future political and monetary union.

Membership of the EU is now 16 countries, all with market economies, and a combined population of some 350 million people. Free movement of goods and capital now make it possible to trade and invest money anywhere in the Union. And free movement of people means that citizens of any EU country can travel, reside, study, and work wherever they wish in the Union.

There are also common agreements on foreign, security, and agricultural policies as well as on justice and domestic affairs issues. The most difficult area is the goal of monetary union—a single European currency and an independent central bank. The only country able to meet all the initial 1995 criteria for a single currency is Luxembourg.

At European Union meetings, the Council of Ministers has a mandate to reach compromises, without any single government being placed at a disadvantage. Proposals for laws are presented to this Council, after being drawn up by the Commission.

The current President of the European Commission is Jacques Santer, a former Prime Minister of Luxembourg. Though a European Parliament plays a steadily increasing role in the drafting of EU laws, it does not yet have the same powers as national parliaments. The Court of Justice ensures that EU law is carried out.

Today Luxembourg is a major supporter and force behind European economic and political unification. Both the Luxembourg government and the people take the issue seriously and understand that there can be no future outside an European Union for a small country like itself. Proof of this commitment can be seen by a 89% voter turnout in recent European elections, compared to only 35% in Britain.

Having full veto power means that, in some circumstances, Luxembourg can veto legislation that commands the support of all the other member states, representing some 350 million Europeans.

*Above:* **The European Union Building.**

*Opposite:* **The European Union of today began with a plan proposed by Frenchman Jean Monnet in 1950 to Robert Schuman (photo). Schuman took up the initiative enthusiastically and pushed hard for the creation of the European Coal and Steel Community a year later.**

# GOVERNMENT

THE STATE OF LUXEMBOURG is a constitutional monarchy. Ultimate power resides with the people through their elected representatives, although there is a hereditary monarch.

If a need arises to consult the people directly on a particular issue of national importance, then a referendum can be held. Results of the referendum, however, are not binding on the government.

## CONSTITUTIONAL RIGHTS

In the first few decades of its independence, Luxembourg went through four different Constitutions. The current one was adopted in 1868 and has been amended several times—in 1919, 1948, 1956, 1972, 1979, 1983, 1988, and 1989—to make the Constitution more democratic. One of the most important amendments was to restrict the monarch's power in the making of laws.

Article 36 of the Constitution now bars the Grand Duke from suspending laws or from dispensing with their enforcement. In theory he sanctions the laws and still could veto anything passed by the Chamber of Deputies, but this veto right has not been used since 1919 and is unlikely to be tolerated in a democratic country.

The Constitution guarantees the rights of citizens and regulates the organization of public authorities. Equality before the law, individual freedom, freedom of opinion and the press, freedom of worship, the right to state education, and the right to work are some of the public rights specified by the Constitution.

*Above:* **Voting is compulsory in Luxembourg's elections. Abstention without justification draws a fine that increases each time the offence is repeated.**

*Opposite:* **A soldier stands guard at the Ducal Palace, residence of the Grand Duke.**

The Chamber of Deputies is the seat of legislative power in Luxembourg. Candidates for election to the Chamber must be at least 21 years old. Voting age, on the other hand, is 18 years.

## *REPRESENTATION OF THE PEOPLE*

For the purpose of general elections the country is divided into four electoral districts. Sixty deputies have been elected every five years by universal suffrage since 1919. Elections of these deputies are based on proportional representation among the various political parties.

Legislative power is in the hands of this 60-member Chamber of Deputies. Legislation is introduced to the Chamber by the executive and when the bill has passed through, it goes to the Grand Duke for signature.

There is also a 21-member advisory body called the Council of State, with members appointed for life by the Grand Duke. This Council of State is not a democratically elected institution and decisions made by them can be overruled. The extent of its power is to delay laws, not to prevent them. Nevertheless, they are required to discuss bills and no final vote can be taken on any bill by the Chamber before the Council's opinion has been heard.

Executive power is exercised by the Council of Ministers, presently 11 Ministers and a Secretary of State, and led by the Prime Minister who is the head of the political party with the most parliamentary seats. The Prime Minister selects Ministers, who are then officially appointed by the Grand Duke, taking care to ensure a cabinet is formed that has the support of the majority of the Chamber. Each Minister is responsible for a particular branch of the public administration. They can speak in the Chamber of Deputies, but they are not members of it. The current prime minister is Jean-Claude Juncker.

A meeting of deputies in progress.

## PUBLIC ADMINISTRATION

The government acts through ministerial departments and public authorities directly answerable to it. Each member of the Government is in charge of one or more ministerial departments, assisted by advisors.

Certain public services, such as tax collection, the post office, and the water authority, are separate from the central offices of the Government. They come under the direction of heads of administration, although still supervised by the minister concerned.

## LOCAL GOVERNMENT

Luxembourg is divided into communes, each administered by a council elected by the people. A majority system is used if the population is under 3,500, and proportional representation where the population is higher. Council members are elected for six years and from their membership an executive body is formed to administer the daily affairs of the commune.

## LAW OF THE LAND

The exercise of judicial power rests with the courts of law and is completely independent of the executive and legislative branches. Judges of the lower courts, Justices of the Peace, are directly appointed by the Grand Duke. These lower courts deal with civil, commercial, and criminal cases of minor importance. Above these are the two District Courts, dealing with civil and criminal cases of greater importance.

The Superior Court of Justice includes both a court of appeal and a Supreme Court. Judges in the Superior Court are chosen by the Grand Duke from a list submitted by members of the high court.

The jury system is not used in Luxembourg. A defendant is acquitted if a majority of the presiding judges find him or her not guilty or there is a division of votes. A Public Prosecutor's department represents the state in the courts and acts under the authority of the Minister of Justice. Assisting them in their work are the police force, responsible for investigating crimes and delivering suspects to the courts, under the supervision of the Attorney-General.

## THE ROYAL FAMILY

The crown of the Grand Duchy is hereditary in the Family of Nassau and passes by lineal descent through the male heir to the exclusion of female heirs. Only failing any male issue in either of the two branches of the family does the crown pass to the female heir of the reigning dynasty. The monarchy is seen by Luxembourgers as a guarantee of stability and

Luxembourg's head of state Grand Duke Jean with his wife Princess Josephine-Charlotte. Grand Duke Jean was trained at Sandhurst, England, served in the British army during World War II, and is still a colonel in a British regiment.

## SYMBOLS OF THE STATE

The Coat of Arms of Luxembourg was decided upon between 1235 and 1239 by Count Henry V with a design of cross bars of silver and blue, and a red lion rampant crowned with gold. On the 23 of June, the national holiday and sovereign's birthday are celebrated. Luxembourg's flag with its three horizontal bands of red, white, and blue is only distinguishable from that of the Netherlands by the shade of its sky-blue as opposed to ultramarine blue.

The National Anthem is the first and last verses of the song *Ons Heemecht* ("ONS he-MEKT") from 1864 with words by the Luxembourger, Micheal Lentz. Far from being a martial song as with many countries, the Luxembourg National Anthem issues a vibrant appeal for peace.

"O Thou above whose powerful hand
Makes States or lays them low,
Protect this Luxembourger land
From foreign yoke and woe.
Your spirit of liberty bestow
On us now as of yore.
Let Freedom's sun in glory glow."

*Luxembourg's national flag is similar to the Netherlands' because from 1815 to 1890, the hereditary rulers of the Netherlands' House of Nassau were also the grand dukes of Luxembourg. The use of the lighter shade of blue was made official only in 1981.*

continuity. Widely admired and popular, the Royal Family live quiet and discreet lives with little pomp or headlines. Far from living an isolated and grand lifestyle, the members of the Royal family can be met shopping in the city center and the youngest generation attend regular primary and secondary schools.

Other reasons for the continued support of the monarchy by the overwhelming majority of the people are nationalistic and economic. Though living in London in exile during World War II, the late Grand Duchess Charlotte spoke to her people regularly on radio and became a living symbol of national identity.

At the end of the war, her husband and son, the present Grand Duke, entered Luxembourg in uniform with the first American liberators. The Grand Duke's involvement in numerous international organizations, and as part of economic missions, also benefits the country's image and results in considerable trade and investment opportunities.

Jean-Claude Juncker became prime minister in 1995 at age 40. He immediately brought a change of style and an infusion of energy to the job. Juncker is admired as a man of great intellect with firm ideas on Luxembourg and its role in the evolving European Union.

## *THE POLITICAL DIVIDE*

Luxembourg has four main political parties: the Christian Social Party (CSP), the Workers Socialist Party (WSP), the Democratic Party (DP), and the Green Alternative Party (GAP)

The Roman Catholic-oriented CSP enjoys popular support and strongly backs NATO. CSP leader and current prime minister, Jean-Claude Juncker, is seen by many Luxembourgers as a relatively young man with new ideas and more dynamism than his predecessor. The DP also has a younger profile since they reacted to a third consecutive election setback by reorganizing, and replacing their president with the popular mayor of Luxembourg City, Lydie Polfer.

The DP is the oldest political party in Luxembourg, drawing support from the professions and urban middle class. It advocates both social legislation and minimum government involvement in the economy and is also pro-NATO. With only 12 seats in the last election and a small membership of 6,500, the DP has virtually found itself shut out of government. The rise of single-issue politics, such as better social security treatment, has made life difficult for the traditional opposition while benefiting those more on the fringe.

Industrial workers who favor strong social legislation support the WSP, which is moderately pro-NATO. The GAP, officially formed in 1983, has built up its parliamentary seats to five because environmental consciousness has grown strongly over the past decade. The Green vote in the European elections was 10% in Luxembourg. The party opposes nuclear weapons and nuclear power as well as Luxembourg's military policies, including its membership in NATO. The rise of the Greens along with the collapse of the communist system in eastern Europe spelled the effective demise of the Communist Party, which lost its one remaining seat in the last election.

When neither of the parties has an absolute majority in Parliament then a coalition government is formed. It has now been over 10 years since the Christian Social Party formed a coalition government with the Workers Socialist Party. Before the 1994 election the press wrote optimistically of fundamental changes and a breakthrough by the Greens. In the end the Socialists and the Social Christians continued in power.

**Colette Flesch (born 1937) studied in France and the United States and is an important member of the Liberal Party.**

## WOMEN IN POLITICS

A number of women have contributed significantly to politics in Luxembourg, with a few achieving high office.

Prominent figures include Colette Flesch and Lydie Polfer. Flesch was Mayor of the City of Luxembourg for 10 years, from 1970–1980. She was also Minister of Foreign Affairs, Minister of Economy, and Minister of Justice during the eighties. In addition to being both Mayor of the City of Luxembourg and President of the Democratic Party, Lydie Polfer is also a member of the European Parliament.

---

### A SMALL ARMY

Luxembourg has no compulsory military service, but as a NATO member it has a contingent of 800 soldiers recruited on a voluntary basis. After three years of voluntary service, recruits leave the army and are guaranteed jobs in the police or postal service. A reserve force can be called up in times of international crisis.

# ECONOMY

ECONOMICALLY, LUXEMBOURG is the most successful country in Europe. It is highly industrialized, with banking, manufacturing, agriculture, and tourism the most important economic sectors. The economy was hit by the global recessions of the 80s and 90s, but the country's production still increased by some 2.7% a year. Luxembourg's per capita GDP is second only to Japan and forecasts are for its economy to continue performing well into the next century. The reasons for the country's prosperity are varied.

## A SUCCESS STORY

The industry and commerce of Luxembourg profit from an ideal geographical location in the center of Europe. This has been exploited to good advantage. Important international cities, as well as major conurbations such as the expanding Saar-Lorraine-Luxembourg region, are situated in the immediate proximity. In the last century, the great transport links with neighboring countries gave impetus to the steel industry, which helped propel Luxembourg to affluence.

Steel from Luxembourg is used all over the world in the building of bridges, skyscrapers, and railways. Liberal taxation laws as well as legally embodied banking secrecy have encouraged the rapid development of the financial center. Social stability has brought the country considerable foreign investment and contributed to the general welfare with unemployment remaining low. Due to many years of prudent financial management, government public debt is minimal.

*Above:* **A worker cleans up at the end of the day.**

*Opposite:* **The Banque et Caisse d'Epargne de l'Etat (BCEE) building in Luxembourg City.**

The construction industry underwent a general decline in the early 1990s.

## WORKFORCE

Luxembourg employs a large number of "cross-border" and foreign workers. Both lower-skilled and highly-skilled labor is recruited, mostly from Belgium, Germany, and France, accounting for 20% of the labor force. The country's unemployment rate is only 2.4%, against the European average of over 10%. The steady increase in employment has, however, slowed in the past few years.

The low unemployment rate is mainly due to a number of public measures to combat unemployment, like early retirement plans and supported training projects for redundant steel workers. Also, the government policy of attracting new firms to settle in Luxembourg, especially in the banking and other service sectors, has been successful.

The economic development of Luxembourg over the last 20 years has been marked by a rapid change in the main types of employment. Focus has shifted to the services sector, such as banking, insurance, distributive trades, and communications. At the same time manufacturing has been diversified.

## SOCIAL CONSENSUS

One of the keys to the economic success story has been social consensus. With so many different nationalities in the country it is often necessary to reach an agreement. The close links which exist between the inhabitants of a small nation make it easier to find solutions on the basis of a national consensus. Although compromise usually costs everyone a little and never makes anyone entirely happy, it seems to have worked as a strategy.

Today, fewer workers are employed in industries like manufacturing. Luxembourg's continued growth will depend on further diversification of its economy into emerging sectors such as media and communications.

For more than 25 years, economic problems have been dealt with by what is known as the "Luxembourg Model." Consultation between the government and employees takes place on many different levels on committees and councils through a tripartite system, involving an official board of employer, trade union, and government representatives. Such a non-confrontational approach to industrial relations and negotiations has so far avoided major disputes.

A general minimum wage to combat poverty has been in existence since 1945. All wage earners benefit from a salary scale whereby each increase of the level of prices leads to an automatic adaptation of salaries, pensions, and allowances. Thus the purchasing power of consumers is safeguarded.

## AN EYE FOR OPPORTUNITIES

Luxembourgers have prospered by being quick to identify opportunities for their economy and exploit market gaps. The banking service, in particular, is a good example. Luxembourg's freedom to maneuver as a tiny state inside the large EU is also important. It can attract business by offering special privileges, which its larger neighbors will not or cannot give.

*At successful Luxembourg companies like Elth S.A., employees work around the clock in shifts so that supplies are made at the moment a part is required.*

Equally important, Luxembourg has elected political leaders who know how to diversify a small economy by attracting investment and finding lucrative service industries, while preserving a good social climate. As a result Luxembourg has, in recent decades, become a pioneer of the Eurobond market; a launch pad for the cable and satellite television business through the lure of deregulation; and a leading personal finance center through customized banking services and tax efficient investment funds. Major international concerns have established new subsidiaries or extended existing plants. Luxembourg is home to an array of Euro-institutions, including the European Court of Justice, the European Investment Bank, the Court of Auditors, the administrative center of the European Parliament, and other lucrative earners clustered together in the city.

## STRIVING FOR QUALITY, SKILL, AND FLEXIBILITY

Because Luxembourg is unable to compete with large producers of consumer goods, it has specialized in market areas where it is important to be the best rather than the largest.

An example is the case of Sisto Armaturen S.A., a company of 90 employees, which concentrates on the manufacture of diaphragm valves, a product that has many applications. Customers admire the exceptional qualities of Sisto products and the small company is now accepted as one of the world's specialists in this field.

Another illustration is the Cerametal Company, which produces hard metal (see picture). With its products so widely distributed there is a good possibility that anyone holding a ballpoint pen at this moment has one with the ball made by Cerametal. The company leads world production, producing 3.5 billion balls a year! It also undertakes intensive research to maintain its technical advantage.

Similarly the thermostat in your washing machine, iron, or vacuum cleaner may well be a product of another Luxembourg company, Elth S.A.

Workers in a school cafeteria. Besides iron and steel, other important branches of manufacturing are metal and machinery, paper and printing, rubber and plastic, and food products.

## *INDUSTRY*

Industry, including mining, manufacturing, and construction, provided 34.9% of GDP and employed almost 30% of the working population in 1993. Iron and steel was once the dominant force in the economy—from the late 19th century until the steel industry crisis in 1975. The industry has, however, now been completely restructured with major cutbacks in jobs. The country's steel company, ARBED, Europe's third largest steelmaker, employed more than 27,000 people in the 1970s. This figure is now nearer 6,000.

This step, accompanied by the thorough modernization of the manufacturing structure, means iron and steel remain the country's main industry, despite dwindling iron resources and reduced demand for Luxembourg's steel exports. ARBED, which remains the country's largest single employer, suffered substantial losses in 1992 and 1993, but returned to profitability in 1994.

A car show in Luxembourg. In addition to the regular events, there are many other shows, such as the Ecology Show, Road Safety, and the Furniture Show.

## *TRADE FAIRS*

Luxembourg has a centuries-old tradition of fairs dating back to the Middle Ages. A central geographical position, financial advantages, and liberal commercial regulations continue to attract merchants from all over Europe.

Annual events are the Spring and Autumn fairs. The Spring fair concentrates on foodstuffs, beverages, sport, and leisure, with some 100,000 visitors. The Autumn fair is devoted to house building, furnishings, craft products, and machines. Valuable antiques, contemporary art, and literary works are also exhibited each year.

Running in parallel with the International Pedigree Dog Show is the Dogexpo, where commercial enterprises present everything required by man for his four-legged friends. Every four years the gastronomic trade show, Expogast, which has gained a coveted international reputation, takes place.

All the fairs and specialized trade exhibitions take place in the huge Trade Fair and Congress Center. This complex contains 24 halls linked by covered passageways, with simultaneous translation facilities, projection rooms, amplification equipment, fax services, parking for 2,500 vehicles, and two restaurants accommodating 800 people. The entire infrastructure is ideal for conferences or trade shows of any kind.

## FINANCIAL SERVICES

The financial service sector, including banking and insurance, contributed 15% of the GDP in 1993. It is the only sector of the economy that sustained economic growth during the global recession. In 1994, there were some 221 banks with a total of 18,954 employees. Over 11,000 holding companies were registered and the stock exchange underwrites more than half of all the Eurobonds issued on the entire European market. Investment portfolio management is also prominent.

One of the main reasons for the growth of Luxembourg as a financial center, apart from the linguistic abilities of Luxembourgers, is the laws concerning taxation. Luxembourg withholds no tax on the interest earned in foreigners' accounts and has strict rules of banking secrecy.

For thousands of wealthy Europeans, who prefer not to pay tax at their country's top rate, it is a pleasant outing to drive to Luxembourg and have a good lunch after visiting the bank. Simpler than a trip to the Cayman Islands and financially safer because Luxembourg is part of a single market with its currency interchangeable with the Belgian franc. Withholding tax is the first wall of the fortress. The inner one is banking secrecy.

All banks in Luxembourg operate under the supervision of the Monetary Institute, the country's equivalent of the central bank. Because Luxembourg is joined in a monetary union with Belgium, the Belgian franc circulates freely in the Grand Duchy at par with Luxembourg bank notes.

*In recent years, Luxembourg has also become a center for the cross-border life insurance industry.*

While banks are obliged to check the origin of funds, they are not compelled to disclose this information, except when judicial procedures have been initiated. All other countries except Luxembourg operate controls on the ability of banks to create money.

These practices, which give Luxembourg its reputation as a tax haven, have prompted other EU countries to try to introduce European legislation to end such tax advantages. The Bank of Credit and Commerce International, based in Luxembourg, was shut down in 1991 by international regulators who believed it was involved in illegal activities. However, any moves to change the laws have always been successfully blocked by Luxembourg, whose revenues substantially depend on the continued profitability of its banks.

## THE EUROPEAN INVESTMENT BANK

The European Investment Bank, based in Luxembourg, finances a broad spectrum of projects, from major infrastructure to small businesses, as long as they further European integration. Its role is bringing people closer together, stimulating trade, and building up links between Europe's regions, while also observing the rules of rigorous banking practice.

Money has been lent, at a fixed-rate and low interest, for major road, motorway, and rail links, air transport, and telecommunications systems across Europe. There has also been funding for advanced technology, such as aeronautical engineering. A large amount of money is funneled to protect the environment, like waste and sewage treatment plants. Last, but not least, are the important energy projects, particularly alternative sources of energy like wind farms.

The Bank maintains a very sound capital base and funds its lending through bond issues.

## AGRICULTURE

Agriculture, including forestry and fishing, contributes only about 2.2% of GDP and employs some 3.0% of the working population. The number of families engaged in agriculture has almost halved in the past 15 years, with a corresponding decline in the number of small farms.

About 92% of land use in Luxembourg is for agricultural purposes and wooded areas. The principal crops are cereals, potatoes, and wine grapes. Substantial numbers of cattle, pigs, and poultry are also raised. The amount of area dedicated to forestry has actually increased over the years and so the production of the main types of trees, coniferous and broadleaved, has also grown. Both imports and exports of raw wood have doubled in 15 years.

Some 1% of the land is used for vine growing. The river valley of the Moselle enjoys a mild climate and ideal soil, lime and clay, which make this region highly suited for producing white wines. It is very similar to the Champagne region of France.

A considerable amount of money is needed to set up a farm and Luxembourgers regard it as a very hard way to make a living, with early mornings and long days.

Seasonal grape picking is performed in the Moselle valley from mid-September to the end of October.

The Luxembourg wine industry rests on two keystones. First the founding of six cooperative cellars between 1921 and 1948. All of these have now combined under an umbrella organization to improve production. Now the vineyard slopes are efficiently cultivated compared to the former small and irregular parcels of land.

Secondly, the authenticity and quality of the wines is guaranteed by a national wine label stamped on every bottle by the state institution of viticulture. This national mark both acts as a stimulus to wine producers to create wines of even higher quality and offers the consumer a guarantee that they are getting a first class wine.

## TOURISM

The spectacular forests and river valleys of Luxembourg are unmatched, in such a small area, anywhere else in Europe. It is the variety, combined with castles, picturesque market towns, sunny vineyards, varied cuisine, and archaeological remains that has fostered the tourist industry.

## ENERGY

Over half of Luxembourg's energy comes from hydroelectric installations, with the rest from thermal power sources. Apart from the two dams on the Upper Sûre River, an important development in this field has been the construction of the hydroelectric power station on the Our River. This station provides electricity during peak hours and its total production of electricity has doubled in 10 years.

Since 1972, large quantities of natural gas have become available, as a result of an agreement with Belgium.

*Because of the steel industry, which uses as much as 90% of the country's total coal consumption, Luxembourg's per capita energy requirement is over twice that of Belgium.*

However, the economic recession in Europe during the 80s and 90s has reduced the number of tourists. People began to find it difficult to afford holidays and, with the brief two month span of the tourist season, this has meant closure for a number of hotels. Another factor is that many visitors prefer the sunny weather of the Mediterranean to the rainy climate of Luxembourg. Such competition close at hand makes it difficult for those working in the tourist industry.

## EXPORTS AND IMPORTS

Luxembourg's principal exports in 1993 were steel, wine, farm produce and manufactures, equipment, and textiles. Main imports were machinery and electrical equipment, base metals, and fuels.

As a small nation with a high standard of living, Luxembourg can only produce a small part of what it requires. Since its production is fairly specialized, it also needs to sell most of the goods and services it produces abroad. Other members of the EU account for most of Luxembourg's foreign trade, with Germany, France, and Belgium the most important trading partners.

Luxembourg and Belgian foreign trade statistics are merged because the two countries are joined in an economic union.

# LUXEMBOURGERS

IN 1995, LUXEMBOURG'S POPULATION totaled an estimated 406,600 people, with an average overall density of 407 people per sq mile (157 per sq km). By European standards this is a reasonable density.

In Europe as a whole, the population density is 160 per sq mile (62 per sq km). As a comparison, crowded Japan has 800 people per sq mile (309 per sq km) and the United States only 50 (19).

Almost three quarters of the population are of working age, between 15 to 64, and slightly over half of the total are female.

## POPULATION TRENDS

The overall trend is a falling birth rate—with the population growing at less than 1% annually—and an aging population. The little growth that has occurred over the last 30 years has only come about because of migration.

Immigrants make up a large proportion of the resident population, 32% in 1993, with over half living in the capital city. A majority of second-generation immigrants adopt Luxembourg nationality.

Since 1967, birth statistics have been drawn up according to nationality. In 1995, the number of births for Luxembourgers was 3,255, with deaths at 3,335. For the immigrant population, births were 2,196 and deaths only 465, partly explained by the fact that many immigrants return to their countries of origin when they retire. As a result the foreign population is much younger than those with Luxembourg nationality.

*Opposite and above:* **The Luxembourger's slightly unconventional character is the result of centuries of intense relations with the culture and people of neighboring nations.**

## *NATIONAL PRIDE*

Luxembourgers are the result of the merging of two quite distinct cultures: in the west, the French group to which Luxembourg is linked by its civilization and in the east, the Germanic group to which the country belongs linguistically. From the end of the third century, migrations of Germanic tribes began settling in the region of Luxembourg. All this resulted in a national identity based on an ability to enrich itself from other cultures and a genuine desire to mix foreign contributions with its own heritage.

Luxembourgers do not fear losing their Luxembourg identity because they see themselves as completely different from the Germans and French. Repeatedly invaded, they have survived and that breeds tremendous loyalty. This national pride and patriotism is easily noticeable today. Delighted to discover the role their nation can play at an international level, as part of a wider Europe, Luxembourgers have gained confidence about their ability as a nation.

## *CHARACTER AND PERSONALITY*

Luxembourgers are known as a friendly, convivial, polite, and open-minded people, who have a well-developed sense of hospitality. Many older Luxembourgers are particularly friendly towards visitors from the United States because of the pivotal role American soldiers played in the liberation of their country from the Nazis.

People in the southern part of Luxembourg also have a reputation for being outspoken. In the north, Luxembourgers are said to have developed an easy-going "joie de vivre" because the harsh living conditions make the locals take advantage of the opportunities offered them as best as they can.

Cautious, hard working, practical, conservative, and traditional: these are traits often associated with the Luxembourger. In addition, Luxembourg entrepreneurs are known for their characteristic self-composure in most situations.

Enjoying the pleasures of life, however, is as important as work, and with a passion for festivities Luxembourgers grasp the opportunity to celebrate and organize processions. The national motto seen carved in stone walls perhaps best sums up the people's character: "We want to remain what we are."

## *MELTING POT*

In terms of ethnic composition, the greatest number of immigrants are Portuguese, Italian, French, Belgian, and German.

The Luxembourgers' ability to compromise can be seen by the successive waves of immigration and the smooth integration of the guest-workers: Italians in 1870s and the 1920s for the steel industry, and the present wave of Portuguese, which began in the 1970s, especially in building and construction. A generally positive attitude to immigrants willing to integrate and form a culturally similar background has produced a melting pot without threatening national identity. The annual "Festival of Immigration" enjoys the

## CAPE VERDE ISLANDERS

Cape Verde, an island nation off the west coast of Africa, and Luxembourg have developed close economic and humanitarian links. In 1993, 11.6 million of the almost 45 million francs of Luxembourg's direct food aid went to the island's population. In fact, the biggest share of all Luxembourg's aid goes to Cape Verde, financing such projects as the renovation of a hospital, provision of water to villages, and building of schools.

In the 1960s, when the first generation of islanders arrived in Luxembourg, Cape Verde was still a Portuguese colony, and did not become independent until 1975. Immigrants went to Portugal first where they were treated as citizens and then to Paris and finally Luxembourg, where there was work. Several thousand immigrants from Cape Verde live in Luxembourg today. Illegal immigration, however, is an ongoing practice, with many living in the country for over 30 years. With adult children in Luxembourg, it is unlikely now that they would return to Cape Verde.

One certainty is that all of the islanders came to the Grand Duchy with the hope of a better life, and for many their emigration has been rewarded.

patronage of the highest dignitaries and the major political parties all emphasize the importance for the country of the presence of non-indigenous people.

In Luxembourg, despite many different nationalities, there has been little, if any, intolerance or racial unrest. Although a group called the "Anti-racism and Anti-Semitism Movement of Luxembourg" does exist, which points to some underlying currents of antagonism, attempts to create extreme-right-wing groups have been very short-lived.

Any fascist notion is fiercely rejected because during World War II Luxembourg suffered greatly in the hands of extremists. Hardly a family has not lost some member in the German concentration camps, on the Russian front, or in the Resistance movement. An important factor that undoubtedly oils this ease of integration is the country's low unemployment rate. Social unrest and conflict are less likely to occur where jobs are plentiful and individuals have some control over their destiny.

The problems faced by immigrants are often more of a practical nature, such as housing shortages and language barriers, which prevent many from

*Opposite and above:* **Because Luxembourg has drawn mostly Catholic migrants, it has managed to retain its religious homogeneity.**

getting ahead, than overt racism. A young man from Cape Verde who works and lives in Luxembourg and is married to a native woman says he experiences no difficulty with the fact that he is black and she white. "Everyone is so friendly to me." The disturbing trend toward a "new poverty" among illegal immigrants living in the country is far more of a threat.

## DRESS

Today it is difficult to find the traditional dress worn anywhere. It is only likely to be seen on festive occasions. The women's traditional dress consists of a full-length, royal-blue skirt, gathered into a waistband and trimmed with a white border above the hem. Worn over this is a small, semi-circular white apron, richly embroidered at the bottom. A long-sleeved, plain white cotton blouse, a red or white cloth bonnet, and a red cloth shawl across the shoulders complete the dress. Flat black shoes and white thick stockings are worn, and a wicker basket is typically carried.

The men's traditional dress is a blue tunic in a smock style with a red edging. Black breeches that reach to the knee are worn, together with a white shirt with either a black bow tie or a red scarf. Long white knee socks, black shoes with silver buckles, and a peaked cap finish off the outfit.

For those living in the rural parts of the country, and earning a living as farmers, the usual costume is a red scarf and short blue overalls. The only other variation is when a dancing routine, an intrinsic part of the culture for women, is performed. On these occasions the usual type of dress is a white blouse with a short black skirt.

The traditional dress makes a rare appearance at this festive dance.

## PROMINENT LUXEMBOURGERS

Despite its small population, Luxembourg has, in recent years, produced several internationally-known personalities.

A figure of national importance was Joseph Bech, Prime Minister during World War II. Bech, a modest and discreet man, played a significant role in keeping up the country's morale during the war years and the consequent turmoil. He also made important contributions to the development of the United Nations and a united Europe, sensitive to the gains from integration rather than focusing on strictly national goals.

Robert Schuman (born in Luxembourg in 1886, died 1963) launched the Schuman Plan that led to the establishment of the European Coal and Steel Community, the first step to European integration. He left Luxembourg to study law in Germany and later lived in France. Elected to the French Parliament in 1919, he fought with the Resistance during World War II and became French Foreign Minister in the late 1940s. Schuman is seen as the architect of European unification and his memory is greatly revered in the country of his birth.

Another Luxembourger, Gabriel Lippmann, was a respected scientist and Physics Nobel Prize winner. Born on August 16, 1845 in a small village, he obtained his doctorate in sciences in Paris in 1875. He then focused his research on thermodynamics and electrical instruments and eventually presented his method of color photography based on the interference of light waves to the French academy. In 1908, he was awarded the Nobel Prize for producing the first color photographic plate, an important first step in the development of color photography.

Following in Lippman's footsteps, prominent modern-day scientists from Luxembourg today include Claude Muller, who has been particularly honored by his fellow scientists. Muller specializes in viral immunology and has received considerable recognition for his work in vaccines.

**Joseph Bech played a prominent role in Luxembourg politics for several decades. He was first elected a Deputy in 1914 and later became the country's Prime Minister.**

# LIFESTYLE

THE VAST MAJORITY OF LUXEMBOURGERS, over 70%, live in towns. Luxembourg society is both urban and very cosmopolitan, something which can sometimes seem at odds with the fact that most of the country's land is used for agriculture.

Although Luxembourg is a small nation, it is not overcrowded. Luxembourgers have ample access to their own space. The pace of life in the capital city can be fast and furious at times, like any other European capital. Away from the city, however, life is slower and more relaxed.

## STANDARD OF LIVING

Luxembourg has the highest standard of living in the EU. Numerous indicators confirm the prosperity of Luxembourg. Citizens of the Grand Duchy receive more social benefits per 1,000 inhabitants than anywhere else in Europe. When prices go up, wages increase accordingly, so consumers do not lose out.

Only the former West Germany has more cars, Denmark more telephones, and the Netherlands more hospitals. Some 70% of Luxembourgers own their homes, and housing standards are high, with all having electricity and running water. Luxembourg has the highest per capita consumption of electricity.

Factors which contribute to a high quality of life are an ideal population density and the absence of big cities. Short distances to and from work, combined with adequate transportation facilities, also help make daily life easier.

*Above and opposite:* **Political stability and economic prosperity have helped make Luxembourg—in the words of former United Nations Secretary-General Perez de Cuellar—"one of the world's happiest nations."**

Most Luxembourgers own their own houses or apartments. Any housing problems are usually those affecting illegal immigrants. However, subsidies are available to help those on low incomes to afford decent housing.

## *HEARTH AND HOME*

Nearly two-thirds of the total population in Luxembourg live in 10 major towns, which are also centers of industrial production. A hundred and fifteen thousand people, about 30% of Luxembourgers, live in just three of these towns. Luxembourg City, the capital, alone has 76,000 inhabitants. Because of exorbitant rents, the center of Luxembourg City sees little activity outside of business hours. Instead, residential areas have sprung up in the vicinity of the city, neatly separated from industrial areas.

In Luxembourg, as in the rest of Europe, the number of people living in rural areas is fast dwindling. Preserving the rural heritage is a difficult task and the delicate balance between town and countryside is in danger. Although the countryside offers much recreational and leisure possibilities, rural areas are unable to sustain a level of economic activity necessary for a dynamic local community. Infrastructure is often poor and services inadequate compared with urban areas.

## COMFORTABLE LIVING

The average Luxembourg family has a detached two to three bedroom house. The size of a house is commonly measured in the amount of space available rather than the number of bedrooms. All have central heating, predominantly oil heat, double glazing, and such features as marble or parquet floors, as a rule of thumb. Gardens and flowers are important to Luxembourgers. For those without a garden, colorful window boxes are next best.

## *FAMILY VALUES*

Luxembourgers have strong traditional values. Families are very important to most people and are a significant part of the social fabric. Boarding schools are a rare sight and every opportunity is taken to spend time with the family—even lunch breaks.

Still, changes are taking place, even in small towns and villages where conservatism and a reluctance to change is often entrenched. As women become more active in working life, many are delaying marriage and children. This is a fundamental change, which other neighboring countries have experienced for much longer. Nevertheless, over 95% of Luxembourg women rate their families as most important in their lives and few place careers before their families.

Making time for the family—such as a weekend stroll in the Place d'Armes, the social center of the capital city—ranks high on the list of priorities for the average Luxembourger.

A student in a hotel school, this young Luxembourger can look forward to a career in the tourism industry after graduation.

## *WOMEN*

Only about 37% of Luxembourg women are in paid employment. However, this is increasing steadily as statistics for "unpaid family workers," measured between the years 1980 and 1994 show, dropping from 20% to 16%. The motivation for working is usually to provide a higher standard of living for the family. A growing proportion of women now provide at least half the household income.

The lack of child-care facilities has prevented the entry of more women into the workforce. At present, there is public provision of child-care services for less than 5% of children up to 3 years old, and Luxembourg is one of only three countries in Western Europe without a statutory paternity allowance.

With the growing dominance of the service industries more job opportunities have been created for women. Nonetheless, women remain under-represented in industry and the professions, despite laws to ensure equal pay and equal access to employment, training, and working conditions.

## YOUNG PEOPLE

Demographic changes mean that in the last 10 years the numbers of youngsters in Luxembourg have been declining. One of the major concerns facing these young people, and this is not unique to Luxembourg, is jobs and careers. Though unemployment is extremely low, a staggering 50% of those unemployed in 1985 were young people aged 16–25.

This was because many young people did not have the necessary vocational qualifications for the labor market. In the late 1970s, a study on the school experience revealed that as many as 40% of young people in the country left the educational system without any formal qualifications As a result, employers were forced to hire workers from other countries.

By 1990, only 25% of job-seekers were under 25, with the change credited to government measures for dealing specifically with hard-to-place job-seekers. There is a training program for young people aged 15 who have left school without any vocational qualifications and who are unemployed. Emphasis is placed on the acquiring of social skills and on helping the young person develop a positive attitude toward work.

While Luxembourgers have managed to fashion a very high standard of living for themselves over the last few decades, the aging population means that younger people will have to bear an increasingly greater burden of maintaining this standard of living.

## *EDUCATION*

Primary education begins at age 6 and lasts for six years. At 12, after taking entrance exams, pupils are allocated to one of three types of schools: grammar, secondary technical, or complementary education. Each of these has different educational and vocational objectives. Education is compulsory until the age of 15.

If a pupil goes to grammar school, and is successful in the final examination at the age of 18–19, they can go on to university. However, Luxembourg does not have its own university, although a Centre Universitaire offers one-year courses in sciences, law, and teacher training. Those who want to study at university must go abroad.

In the secondary technical system, a student can stay until 18, leaving with a vocational qualification, an apprenticeship, or a diploma for higher technical studies.

The complementary education course is for those students who fail to get into either of the mainstream options. Complementary education classes have come under considerable criticism because they offer poor chances for qualifications and are attended by low-achievers, many of whom are young immigrants.

In 1991, about 28% of the government's annual expenditure was channeled into social security services for Luxembourgers.

Children with a disability receive special education, separate from the mainstream. Many parents disagree with this, believing that their disabled child would benefit from being educated alongside the able-bodied.

## THE WELFARE STATE

The low birth rate, relative to the aging population, is of acute concern to those responsible for government policy. Average life expectancy has risen from 50 in 1900 to 72 for men and 79 for women by 1995. The result: growing numbers of elderly people, but fewer people of working age to provide for them.

Economic consequences include increases to the state burden of old age pensions and sickness benefits. Political consequences arise from finding the money to pay for these growing costs. Thus far the welfare state in Luxembourg has survived attempts to cut benefits. Indeed, any move to do so would be very unpopular with the voters.

Social policies are highly developed. All types of employment are subject to compulsory contributory benefits, which is a combination of taxes paid by employees and employers. The resulting comprehensive social insurance plan covers medical and hospital treatment, invalidity and old-age pensions, family allowances, and unemployment benefit. A major advantage of this system is that everyone receives health care benefits, unlike in the United States, where only the poor receive help. Hospital treatment is free, but those who can afford better treatment, for example, less time waiting for an operation, are free to take private medical insurance. The number of general physicians, specialists, and hospital beds available have all increased substantially during the last decade.

The family allowance, which most industrialized countries have, with the notable exception of the United States, is a universal cash benefit that goes to every family regardless of income. The government itself does not operate social services. They are run by public bodies made up of representatives of the government, and employers and employees.

## CRIME AND PUNISHMENT

The police in Luxembourg, as in all European countries except Britain, are armed, but their presence on the streets is not a heavy one. Relationships between the public and the police are generally good and the powers they possess are not viewed as particularly interfering or excessive.

For the average law-abiding citizen, the offence most likely to give them food for thought is driving under the influence of alcohol. The maximum permissible blood-alcohol concentration is 80 mg, about 2 units, and penalties are high for those who go above this. It can lead to a severe fine, loss of a driver's license for a year, and sometimes imprisonment.

The lifting of borders has affected crime rates at all levels. Drug-related crime, prostitution, burglaries, and muggings are all increasing, but statistics for violent crime remain at the same level.

Police officers provide a reassuring presence on the streets. A total of 43 murders in 1989 gave the tiny state a homicide rate of 11.8 per 100,000 people, three times the rate of any other European country. On the whole the native population has not become more criminal, but international crime has infiltrated the country, attracted by its cosmopolitan atmosphere and its conspicuous wealth. In Luxembourg's central prison, most inmates are foreigners awaiting extradition.

A gaily-colored recycling bin—one of the many bins that can be found around the country. Luxembourgers value their environment, controlling development and preserving rural landscape. Over one-fifth of Luxembourg's total land area is protected, compared to less than 9% in the United States.

## GREEN LIVING

Much of Luxembourg's charm lies in the variety of its scenery and the many country areas available for leisure pursuits. Citizens are careful about their surroundings and litter is rarely, if ever, seen on streets. But industrialization has caused damage to the environment and people living in the capital and alongside the motorways are particularly troubled by noise pollution.

The high density of motor vehicle traffic and the concentration of industry leads to high levels of nitrogen oxides in the air and significant dustfalls. Air pollution remains below the critical health threshold, but effects on human health and that of the forests are coming under careful scrutiny. Acid rain is damaging the forests.

Conditions of most rivers are acceptable, but some watercourses, about 4% of the total, in the center and south of the country, are quite heavily polluted. Estuaries, in particular, bear the brunt of man's carelessness. Quality of the drinking water is generally satisfactory, but groundwater in some aquifers is under threat, both from an increase in nitrates and decreasing amounts available.

## ENVIRONMENTAL PLANNING

In recent years public opinion has swung dramatically in favor of a more dynamic environmental policy and, through special interest groups, pressure is being consistently applied. The Green Alternative Party has been an influential force in national affairs to the extent that the majority of Luxembourgers are willing to forgo higher living standards if it means keeping their country clean. Environmental politics have come of age with the authorities trying to introduce a more comprehensive approach to environmental planning in order to counter the most pressing threats.

Pollution from Luxembourg's factories. The country now has almost 40 monitoring sites measuring the amount of nitrogen dioxide in the air. By comparison, this is double the number Great Britain—a much larger country—has.

*Any large agricultural projects requiring aid from EU common funds are now subject to environmental impact assessments. There are also in place various restrictions regarding new zones of economic activity.*

### FREE COMPOST FOR RUBBISH

Luxembourg was one of the first European countries to split up rubbish into three kinds: organic, plastics, and general. Recycling bins for batteries, medicines, and clothes as well as the usual glass and paper are common. One innovative and popular recycling measure is free compost made from local garbage.

A resident can visit the nearest local commercial compost dump and obtain free compost for a garden or balcony. The compost is produced from that residential area's garbage so, in essence, the resident is getting back his or her garbage, but in a useful form!

# RELIGION

IN THE PAST, RELIGION WAS AS DIVISIVE an issue in Luxembourg as in the rest of Europe. Many battles and massacres took place in the name of religion. Today, over 95% of Luxembourgers are Roman Catholic, and any discrimination on the basis of religion is illegal. Luxembourgers remain deeply committed to Catholicism and their religion is still an important part of their cultural life.

## *FROM DRUIDS TO CHRISTIANITY*

The Druids were a priestly order who ruled in this area until Roman law, and later Christianity, put an end to their dominance. Little is known about the Druids, other than they were part of an elaborate religious and political organization. Their religion was a cult of numerous gods and natural objects, such as trees and water, in which magical practices were involved. Assemblies were held in consecrated spots, such as groves of oaks. Mistletoe growing on these oaks was venerated and used in medicine. The Druids wielded great political as well as religious power, and all who refused to obey were slain.

Christianity was introduced early in Luxembourg during the third century, but only began to flourish in the seventh with the arrival of Irish and English missionaries. It was the Anglo-Saxon priest, St. Willibrord, who converted all of the Low Countries to Christianity. He worked for many years from Echternach, from which he spread the message of Catholicism throughout the region. St. Willibrord was buried in Echternach, where his crypt still stands. His tomb became one of the most important pilgrimage goals in the region, with many believing that the influence from the altar of the crypt could cure the plague, leprosy, and eye afflictions.

*Above:* **A hand-colored engraving of Druids harvesting mistletoe to use in their ceremonies, while Roman soldiers keep watch. Today's Christmas tradition of putting up mistletoe dates back to Druid traditions.**

*Opposite:* **The imposing entrance to St. Mary's Cathedral.**

A medieval engraving of a monk copying a manuscript.

## A MEDIEVAL CENTER

During the Middle Ages, learning was concentrated in the large monastic centers, where monks preserved important books by carefully copying them, adding often elaborate illustration. Most of this work of copying was concentrated on the gospels.

One of the most important monastic centers during the early Middle Ages was Echternach. It is remembered today chiefly for the Echternach Gospels, lavishly decorated 11th-century manuscripts that are one of the best examples of Ottonian manuscript illumination.

The old Benedictine Abbey that still stands in Echternach was founded in the seventh century by St. Willibrord. Known as the Basilica because of its resemblance to the one in Rome, it has four wings of 230 feet (70 m) built around a large square courtyard. One of the most important religious buildings in the country, it houses a magnificent white sarcophagus with the remains of St. Willibrord.

## THE PROTESTANT CHALLENGE

During the Middle Ages, all of Europe was Catholic. But with the spread of the Reformation in the late 15th and early 16th centuries, Protestant beliefs and practices began to spread and slowly dominate. The Reformation, an attempt to reform the Catholic Church, was begun by Martin Luther in 1517. Luther's attacks on issues of doctrine and the widespread corruption within the Catholic Church changed religious practices in Europe. Many breakaway sects grew rapidly and took up revolutionary views, particularly a militant Protestantism called Calvinism.

The Spaniards, who ruled the Low Countries at this time, were staunch defenders of the Catholic faith. This was the time of the brutal Inquisition in Spain, when no torture was too terrible. Widespread resentment at the Spaniards' attempt to hold their subjects submissive to the Catholic Church grew as Protestantism become firmly entrenched elsewhere.

Religious differences flared up between the north and south of the Low Countries, with the south (present-day Luxembourg and Belgium) alarmed at the spread of Lutheranism and Calvinism. The new Protestant doctrines failed to penetrate Luxembourg's borders, which remained Catholic and loyal to Spain. The north, today's Netherlands, became Protestant. All over Europe, rulers had to decide whether to accept or reject this new religion, and this split between Catholicism and Protestantism ravaged Europe for over a century.

*In 1626 there were 15,544 Jesuits worldwide. This increased to 22,589 by 1749. The society's founder, Ignatius, died in 1556.*

## JESUIT ORDER

The Roman Catholic order of religious men founded by St. Ignatius in 1540 has been noted for its educational, missionary, and charitable works in modern times. St. Ignatius was a Spanish soldier who experienced a religious conversion and established the order.

The society grew rapidly and assumed a prominent role, thus exposing it to much hostility. Education and scholarships were the principal work from the beginning. Early Jesuits were also preachers, many entering the foreign missionary field, and were often called upon to be confessors to many of the royal families within Europe.

Jesuits have always been controversial. While some have seen them as the most esteemed religious order, others have regarded them as something to be feared and condemned. Certainly in the 15th and 16th centuries, their efforts to be the predominant religious power contributed to the witch hunts and burnings of this period.

## *WITCHCRAFT*

In the Duchy between 1588 and 1631, as many as 100 women were victims of witch trials annually. Some men were also accused of this crime. All that was needed to set the machinery going was a rumor, and often these rumors pointed to women living alone and isolated from society, who were felt to be suspicious characters. The ordinances of Philip II of Spain laid down strict procedures in the matter of interrogation and torture. Everything had to be done "through legitimate legal procedures according to the principles of law, honesty, reason, and justice."

After about 1631, the trials stopped in Luxembourg. Work began on the building of a new society based on law and order, and witchcraft was no longer a preoccupation of the judges.

### TRIAL AND EXECUTION

Once a trial was underway, new accusations against new suspects were provoked under torture. The accused witch would have her vengeance on those who made her suffer by denouncing them as accomplices. Often the charges boiled down to a case of bad reputation and the interpretation of odd behavior. Perhaps the woman was heard at night letting out awful shrieks, or her sister-in-law accused her of killing one of her babies by looking at it.

Acquittal came if one withstood the torture without confessing, but then very often the accused died afterwards from the torture. If one did not confess, then there was no proof. The ritual of execution was the crowning glory of the whole system. Witchcraft was considered one of the most heinous crimes against God and the king, and the judges needed the spectacle of the stake to reveal the person's guilt. Everyone had to see the body burning in order to identify with the triumph of law. All joined in the execution, with the villagers gathering firewood. On the assigned day, a procession of the entire population conducted the prisoner to death. Often the person was strangled by the executioner before being completely reduced to ashes. A banquet followed for the local lords and magistrates.

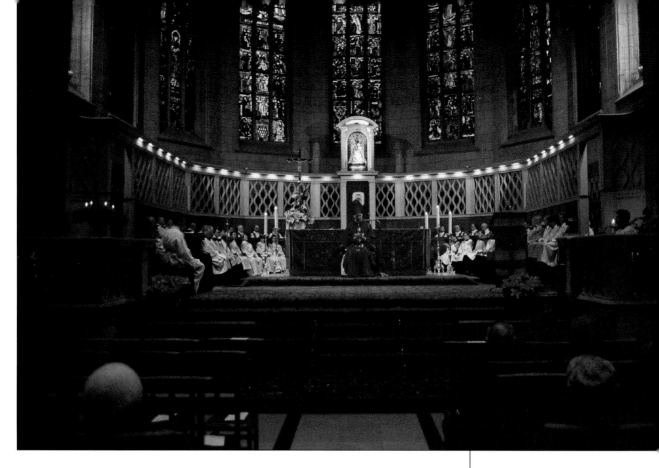

## *RELIGION TODAY*

Today the population is overwhelmingly Roman Catholic. When the pope visited the country in 1980, the bishop was elevated to archbishop and placed under the direct authority of the pope, without any intermediate hierarchy. This is an almost unprecedented occurrence, an illustration of how important Luxembourg is to the Catholic Church.

Almost all Protestant churches are represented in Luxembourg, though their influence is small. The Evangelical faith has the most followers. There is a notable Jewish community as well.

In Luxembourg, as in most countries in the West, there has been a dramatic fall in the number of people, especially young adults, who attend a church of any denomination. Despite the influence of the Catholic Church, the birth rate is one of the lowest in the world, and the number of divorces has soared. Recruitment of clergy, like church attendance, is also decreasing rapidly. However, the Church still holds an important place in the lives of most Luxembourgers.

It is during the fortnight of the national pilgrimage, the Octave, beginning on the third Sunday after Easter, that the Cathedral Notre Dame becomes the center of religious life in the country. During these two weeks, large numbers of Luxembourgers flock here to venerate the image of Our Lady, patron saint of the city.

*Opposite.* A 1489 woodcut of witches conjuring up a hailstorm.

Despite a decline in church attendance among young people, politics and religion are deeply mixed and the church dominates many facets of life, including the media and education. The conservative party is intimately linked with the Catholic Church. The daily paper, the *Luxemburger Wort*, is the official publication of the Christian Social Party and the Catholic Church. The royal family are all devout Catholics.

Relations between the State and the Church are governed by law. All clergy of the officially recognized churches are paid by the State, giving them a civil service status, although they are appointed by the religious authority. Religion is a compulsory subject in schools, although a special course on morals and social studies was introduced as an alternative some years ago. School holidays are centered on and determined by religious holidays.

## PLACES OF WORSHIP

A main center for Luxembourg's Catholics is the Cathedral of Our Lady, known as the Cathedral Notre Dame. Built as a Jesuit church in 1613, in the Gothic manner with a Renaissance door, it was extended in 1935 with the addition of impressive spires. Noteworthy inside are the massive pillars, with very original ornamentation, and magnificent sculptures and statues.

There is also a crypt containing the burial vaults of various members of the Grand Ducal family and important bishops. Access to the crypt, with 12 columns supporting the church above, is by a staircase guarded by two bronze lions bearing the arms of the House of Luxembourg.

Other places of worship in the capital city include the church of St. Michael from the 10th century, the chapel of St. Quirin (14th century), the church of St. Jean upon the Stone (17th century), and the Protestant church from the 18th century.

*For many centuries, sarcophagi (or stone coffins) were the main form of internment for a person who had died. The word sarcophagus comes from Greek words, meaning "flesh" and "eat." During the rule of the Roman Empire, the coffins were carved on the sides with various pictures, usually of battles. On the lid was carved the recumbent figure of the deceased.*

Outside the city center the country is full of churches and chapels. The most prominent ones are in the north, such as in the village of Heiderscheidergrunt. The chapel here has a unique octagonal shape called an "inkpot." Built in 1850, it is dedicated to St. Kinigunde, who is represented in a statue above the door, and has his image painted in a stained-glass window. Inside the chapel, in the town of Esch-sur-Sûre, there is an imposing life-size carving of the Gothic Calvary (Christ on the cross with the two thieves). It is one of the most important cultural treasures of the country.

At another village, called Bavigne, a chapel to Our Lady was built in honor of a pledge the villagers made if they survived Nazi occupation. Since 1953 the hilltop behind the town has been dominated by three huge oak crosses and the chapel, with a valuable statue of Our Lady on a stone pedestal. Echternach remains an important religious center. An open-air mass is celebrated at Echternach each year on Whit Sunday to venerate the relics of St. Willibrord.

**The Cathedral Notre Dame's three spires are today a landmark on the city's skyline. Among those buried within the cathedral's crypt is the revered 14th century Count of Luxembourg, John the Blind.**

*The parish church at Vianden, recently renovated, was built in 1248 in the Gothic style with two naves.*

# LANGUAGE

THE NATIONAL LANGUAGE OF LUXEMBOURG is Luxembourgish ("LUX-em-borg-gish"), or Letzenburgish ("LET-zen-borg-ish"). Like the Flemish language, it is an offshoot of one of the many branches of Germanic languages. Luxembourgers, however, do not like it to be confused with German.

During the Nazi occupation in 1941, the people voted by an overwhelming 96% in a referendum to convey to their oppressors that their language was not German, but Luxembourgish. After the war the public use of Luxembourgish increased dramatically as a natural reaction against four years of suppression. It eventually came to win its full right of use in the Grand Duchy.

*Above:* A signboard warns passersby of danger from lightning in four languages.

*Opposite:* **By birth the Luxembourger is monolingual and only speaks his or her native Luxembourgish. It is education that makes him or her trilingual or more.**

As a country straddling the linguistic frontier, Luxembourg has always represented a meeting place of the cultures and political worlds, both of France and Germany. Not surprisingly then, as a result, French and German are spoken fluently alongside the national language. Each language has a different function within the Luxembourg society.

## RIVALRY OF LANGUAGES

While naturally proud of their own language, Luxembourgers realize they are in a unique position, where French and German are equally important. Still, they consider it common courtesy to try to speak the national language of a country, especially when working there.

Consequently, anger is sometimes felt when workers from across the border, and even those actually living in Luxembourg, consistently refuse to learn and speak the most basic Luxembourgish words.

A student looks up the school notice board for the latest sports updates, written in Luxembourgish and French. In primary school, children learn to read and write in German. French is not taught until the second year of primary education and does not become the main language of instruction until the fourth year of secondary school. Scientific subjects remain taught in German throughout a student's life.

Luxembourgish was only granted the status of a full-scale national language in 1984, with grammar and spelling finally decided upon. However, it has not been able to replace the use of German or French in written communication. French is generally used for administrative purposes, while German is used in other areas, such as religion.

For many people, mastering one language can be difficult, yet the citizens of Luxembourg learn three in school. In addition, English is also commonly used. Nevertheless, it is important to realize that Luxembourgers, though justifiably proud of their ability to be trilingual, are not native speakers of French or German.

## THREE LANGUAGES, THREE USES

The Luxembourgish language is the language used in everyday life within the family and at every level of society. Spoken by just over 400,000 people in the entire world, it is estimated that 25,000 of these are descendants of the émigrés from the late 19th century, now living in the United States. All Luxembourgers speak Luxembourgish at home. This no longer implies an association with the working or uneducated classes as in the past. First and second generation immigrants speak the language of their country of origin. In the workplace Luxembourgers speak Luxembourgish amongst themselves, but communicate either in French or German with cross-border workers.

In public life, official notices from the government and the administration are drawn up in French, but the use of Luxembourgish is becoming more widespread. The Grand Duke and the Ministers, for example, now always address the nation in Luxembourgish. Justice in the courtroom is dispensed almost exclusively in French, but witnesses may speak in their mother tongue to avoid misunderstanding. For legal contracts, German and French are the only authorized languages. Advertisements are usually bilingual, but the use of Luxembourgish is significantly increasing. Cinemas generally screen films in their original language, with French and sometimes German subtitles. The Catholic Church uses German in the majority of its written communications, while sermons are spoken more and more often in Luxembourgish. At school, Luxembourgish, introduced 80 years ago as an independent subject, is the language of instruction in preschool education from age 4 to 6.

A class in progress. An educational system based on German until a student is 15 or 16 can prove problematic for immigrant children speaking Latin tongues like Portuguese. As a result there have been moves to introduce French as the principal language from the first year of primary school.

## *LUXEMBOURGISH IN THE ARTS*

Although a fair amount of classical and modern literature has been written in Luxembourgish, little of it is well-known outside the country. Much of this work is based on themes common to European literature and then adapted to Luxembourg life.

Humor and satire are key ingredients. Still, despite only 400,000 speakers of the language, literary publishing in Luxembourgish is thriving.

Luxembourgish theater is very popular. All villages or towns with more than 300 inhabitants put on at least one theatrical performance a year. An occasional feature film and a number of shorts testify to the viability of a small but high quality film industry.

### *AN AMERIKA*: A POPULAR LUXEMBOURGISH SONG

Edmond Lentz, a 19th-century writer in Luxembourgish, described the sadness of an emigrant who, now in United States, recalls the charms of his former homeland.

"From my village I came over here,
which lies deep in the country-green
over there beyond the big ocean—
so far from me, so far;
There stands a poor and tiny house,
a bench before the door,
There a lime-tree spreads its leaves
and gives it a shadowy coolness.
How deeply aches my heart,
Give me back my cottage roof
I'd give my life's blood for it."

## STANDARDIZING LUXEMBOURGISH

An official dictionary was introduced in 1950 after several inconclusive attempts to standardize the spelling of written Luxembourgish. Over the years official government circulars on spelling have been issued, with the last one in 1976. This is a rare example of where a legislative measure has succeeded in imposing regularity in a previously chaotic linguistic field.

One of the characteristics of the dialect is the absence of rules and norms, so there is not really a uniform language spoken all over. An exception to this lack of rules is the use of the second person singular, when the person being addressed is known, and the second person plural, when the occasion is more formal.

*Above and opposite:* **Despite huge strides in the use of Luxembourgish within the country, Luxembourgish is presently not an official language of the European Union. Nor is it a working language of the European institutions.**

Young immigrants pick up the basics of Luxembourgish in class.

## *LEARNING LUXEMBOURGISH*

For such a small country there is a staggering number of local and regional variations of the language. Pronunciation varies greatly within a few miles. In the south the language sounds like a form of brogue, while in the north there is a pure pronunciation of vowels.

Because the dialect is Germanic, many everyday words are German. Due to the influence of French culture, as many as 1,000 French words are used in everyday language as well, for example, "Gare" ("GAR," station)

There are many "x" sounds in Luxembourgish and "w" is always pronounced as "v". Nouns are spelled with capital letters, but grammar is completely different, depending on where one lives. The plural of the word man is *Maenner*("MEN-er") in the south and *Men*, as in English, in the north.

A conversation between Luxembourgers is likely to be peppered with Luxembourgish, French, and German phrases, and perhaps even some English!

*Surnames are usually Germanic, or occasionally Latin, which was at some point adopted to point out the difference between Luxembourg and Germany during the country's occupation. The most popular names are "Muller" ("MULL-er," meaning miller), "Weber" ("WEB-er," meaning weaver), "Schmit" ("SCH-mit," meaning smith), and "Schumacher" ("shoe-MA-her," meaning shoemaker).*

To greet someone, Luxembourgers say *Moien* ("MOY-en," hello). If inquiring about a person's health, one would say, *Wei geet et deriech* ("Vee geet et der-reich," how are you?). Polite phrases, such as *Wann ech gelifft* ("vun ECK gel-liff," please), and *Merci* ("mare-SEE," thanks), are useful words to know.

## POPULAR NAMES

A person with a French first name and a Germanic-sounding surname is likely to be from Luxembourg. Because French has been the official written language for so long, Luxembourgers all tend to have French first names with a Luxembourgish equivalent. A common name for a boy— "Pierre"—will also be expressed as "Pier" ("PE-air"). Other typical Christian names for boys are "Jang" ("uu-NG," John), and "Maett" ("MAT," Matthew). Popular names for girls are "Marechen" ("MA-re-hen," Marie) and "Therese" ("TER-es," Theresa). This custom of French first names is changing with the rapidly growing immigrant population.

## *BROADCASTING AND NEWSPAPERS*

Luxembourg lies at the crossroads of Europe, and residents can easily access French, German, Belgian, and Italian television. Within Luxembourg, the privately-owned CLT Multi Media runs nine television stations as well as 13 radio stations offering services in Luxembourgish, French, German, English, Dutch, and Italian. Radio Luxembourg, a famous station that operated for nearly 60 years with a huge influence on British popular culture, went off the air in 1991 (see box).

Another group, the Luxembourg-based consortium SES, operates four television satellites—the first of which, ASTRA 1A, was launched in 1988—broadcasting 64 channels to a pan-European audience. It also operates 46 radio stations.

## WHEN RADIO LUXEMBOURG RULED THE WAVES

When the British Broadcasting Company (BBC) held a monopoly over radio broadcasting in the 1930s, the British public had a very limited choice of programs. Launched in 1933, the Luxembourg station, Radio Luxembourg, built a huge transmitter to reach British audiences. Programs were based on British-recorded dance music and advertisements, ironically made in London, and then sent over to be broadcast from Luxembourg. It was the first station to give people what they wanted rather than what it was thought they should have. A major diplomatic dispute broke out between the BBC and Radio Luxembourg over this, but the station proved to be a huge success and stayed on the air 24 hours a day for almost 60 years, interrupted only by World War II.

Radio Luxembourg was a very international station with German, French, and English services, and even a few weekly broadcasts in Luxembourgish. The English service, broadcast on 208 medium wave transmissions, came to symbolize nonstop pop music with about two million British listeners. The first Beatles record ever heard on radio was played on Radio Luxembourg in 1962—*Love Me Do.*

The last words to listeners when Radio Luxembourg went off the air in 1991 were the same that had been used for half a century: "Goodnight, good listening, and goodbye."

One of the more famous Radio Luxembourg disc jockeys was Captain Peter Townsend, who fell in love with a British royal, Princess Margaret, in 1955. Because he was not a royal himself, and would have had to obtain a divorce in order to marry Margaret, the relationship was constitutionally barred, which saddened millions of people all over the world. The princess and the captain decided to end their relationship and, sadly, never met again.

*According to 1992 UNESCO figures, Luxembourg has nearly a quarter of a million radio receivers and over 100,000 television receivers.*

In addition, environmental groups and groups representing foreigners residing in Luxembourg also have their own radio stations.

The only English language newspaper is the weekly *Luxembourg News.* There are five daily newspapers and, with 358 newspapers per 1,000 people printed, Luxembourg has one of the highest newspaper readerships in the world. The largest of the dailies, *Luxemburger Wort,* publishes in German and French, and has a circulation of over 80,000.

# ARTS

LUXEMBOURGERS ARE THE BENEFICIARIES of a rich cultural cross-fertilization. The considerable number of immigrants, European Union civil servants living and working in Luxembourg, as well as the international banking sector, has given birth to a plethora of national and regional culture associations from all over Europe. With more than a fifth of the population non-Luxembourgers, the country resembles a miniature Europe.

## ARCHAEOLOGY

Very few archaeological sites were found in Luxembourg until 1991, with the discovery of Bastendorf, a Celtic place of worship in the Ardennes. Extensive excavations revealed that the shrine was in use from the first century B.C. until the second half of the third century when it was abandoned during an invasion.

Situated close to water, which was considered a life-giving element with access to the underworld, the shrine disclosed many offerings of silver coins and jewelry, a common method in that age of expressing gratitude or anxiety. Most notable was the find of curse boards, small lead tablets folded in such a way that the five-line curse would not be visible. Placed in the stream bed of the shrine, these curses would then be fulfilled by the gods of the underworld. It is thought that there were regular gatherings at Bastendorf for religious festivals with the sacrifice of animals. The exact god likely to have been worshipped is not clear.

*Opposite:* **One of the many works of art found around the country—a fountain sculpture of children with their sheep, sheltering from the rain.**

*Below:* **The Roman period section of the National Art and History Museum.**

*Until the discovery at Vichten, only four of the original 46 Roman Muse mosaics thought to be in the Low Countries had been found. Archaeologists believe the excellent state of the mosaic is due to a landslide, which covered the land with a layer of clay.*

In 1995, another important archaeological discovery was made. A farmer, from the town of Vichten in the north, discovered by chance a 72 yard (60 m) square Roman mosaic on his land. The floor mosaic represented the nine muses—"mountain women"—which, in Greek mythology, are the daughters of the great gods Zeus and Mnemosyne. The find, dated at A.D. 240, has proved to be one of the largest and best preserved mosaic works of its kind north of the Alps.

Although other archaeological sites in Luxembourg are minor and comparatively little known, they are, nevertheless, of interest and many have the additional merit of lying off the beaten track. There are the Roman baths near the town of Mamer and four other sites lying north from the capital city. Another site of interest is the Gallo-Roman complex at Echternach, on the Sûre River, developed between A.D. 50 and A.D. 400. What is seen today are the reconstructed lower sections, although some of the original stonework is still visible. The extensive Roman remains lie alongside medieval ramparts and an eighth century abbey founded by the first Anglo-Saxon missionary working on the continent, St. Willibrord.

A display of souvenirs targeted at visitors.

## TRADITIONAL CRAFTS

Most of the traditional crafts have long been abandoned because the Luxembourg market is too small to withstand foreign industrial production. The one remaining craft, pottery making, is a very small industry.

A recent trendy development is a type of craft popular with tourists and increasingly on display at the different town markets. An example is the "Peckvillercher," small earthenware birds used as whistles, and given by young lovers as presents.

## THEATER AND CINEMA

A new theater building was built in 1964, with one hall seating 1,000 people and an auditorium for 600 people. During the annual theater season, an international festival of operas, plays, concerts, and ballets with multicultural themes, are held. Luxembourg is also a regular stop for many theater touring companies and so is the beneficiary of various types of plays and social commentaries.

The city of Wiltz in the Ardennes is the setting for the open air International Theater Festival in the castle's amphitheatre. Each year in July, world-famous actors perform in front of spectators from all over Europe.

The Centre National de l'Audiovisuel (CNA) has copies of films made in the last 100 years. This provides a history of filmmaking in Luxembourg and introduces four men who played pioneering roles in bringing cinema to the Grand Duchy: Rene Leclere, Evy Friedrich, Pierre Bertogne, and Phillipe Schneider. The first film ever made here was shot in 1899, four years after the Lumiere brothers in Paris projected the world's first public films. An annual film festival shows many new short films, which are directed by new Luxembourg talents.

Luxembourg is the home to an increasing number of production companies. Moves by the Ministry responsible have resulted in foreign film and television producers transferring some of their activities to Luxembourg. Luxembourg supports increased spending on media development, but opposes keeping European cinema and television screens free of American imports, which many countries want in order to promote European culture.

The theatergoing audience in Luxembourg is sophisticated in its tastes and appreciates compassionate writing, poetic language, and outstanding acting, regardless of its country of origin.

## *MUSIC*

Luxembourg has a symphony and a chamber orchestra. Concerts are held regularly throughout the year at the Conservatory of Music in the city suburbs. Classical music is very popular with Luxembourgers, with good support for the chamber orchestra, the European Soloists Luxembourg.

Folk music in Luxembourg is provided mainly by Guy Schons and his group, *Dullemajik* ("duu-le-MA-jik"). At a time when many artists use the latest forms of contemporary music to attract their audience, Schons prefers to draw on the repertoire of old classics, but updated in his own way.

*Dullemajik* attracts leading singers and musicians, particularly renowned accordionist Maurizio Spiridigliozzi and singer Alexandra Ley. There are also bagpipe, flute, and guitar players in the group, whose fame has crossed national boundaries. And, of course, the hurdy-gurdy, an ancient string instrument used to accompany popular songs and dance and still used in Luxembourg in the 19th century, played by Schons.

Although traditional music still commands a following in Luxembourg, the average young music fan is influenced by the international pop charts, featuring American and English rock and pop, and the satellite television stations available.

## THE EUROPEAN SOLOISTS LUXEMBOURG

The European Soloists Luxembourg is a two-year-old ensemble. It unites the best musicians, from famous European orchestras, into a top-class chamber orchestra under the direction of the Slovakian violinist and conductor, Jack Handler. "Music comes from the heart and is a means of communication," Handler explains.

The orchestra has found a home in the north of Luxembourg, where rehearsals are held. Supported by many patrons, including members of the Grand Ducal family, it has given many concerts in Luxembourg, as well as other European cities, such as Frankfurt, Budapest, and Paris.

## PAINTING AND SCULPTURE

Unlike many European countries, the reputation of Luxembourgish artists is not an international one. But while there are no great masters from a past age whose achievements can be celebrated or paintings hung on gallery walls, Luxembourg has produced a number of artists who deserve recognition.

Born in St. Hubert in the Ardennes in the 17th century, Pierre Redoute began at the age of 13 a career that was to make him the most influential botanical artist of all time. In Paris, he worked for the Emperor Napoleon's wife, Josephine, creating over 600 vellum drawings that are still studied today.

Jos Sunnen, who lived from 1894–1982, was a classic exponent of the Impressionistic style of painting. Frantz Seimetz (1858–1934) painted as a naturalist. Joseph Kutter, also from the 19th century, was an expressionist painter who introduced modern art to Luxembourg. Nico Klopp, a famous expressionist painter, born in 1894, contributed greatly to the world of art.

In the capital city, sculptures can be found around many public buildings.

*The main frontage of the capital's Municipal Palace, the administrative home of Luxembourg, bears a sculpture by Pierre Federspiel. This represents the Countess Ermesinde presenting the charter of freedom to the citizens of Luxembourg in 1244.*

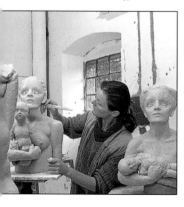

## NICO KLOPP

Nico Klopp, the son of a wine-grower on the Moselle, studied at the Royal Prussian Academy of Art in Dusseldorf. In Dusseldorf, Nico met his future wife and produced his first expressionist woodcuts. Eventually, separated from his wife and daughter, he returned to Luxembourg and survived with paintings, preparing illustrations for periodicals, and by rearing rabbits! Despite living in a small town in the Moselle, where artists were not admired, he never gave up painting and engraving. Ultimately, forced by his financial circumstances, he became a local tax collector.

The first paintings by Nico Klopp were characterized by tragic romanticism. Later works were even more severe, but with a splendid power of light. Often Nico's work met with severe criticism at home. It led to debates between art critics who defended classical academic art, and those who espoused the avant-garde modern school of expressionism, as represented by Nico Klopp. Nico himself never took up the battle in the name of his art, although he was a driving force behind the organization of the first "secessionist" exhibition in Luxembourg in 1927. Significantly this was 63 years after exhibitions in Paris of Manet and others.

The sole demand that Nico made was the recognition of his artistic work. For him beauty was the only purpose of art and he broke with academic prerequisites and rules, which at that time were the only criteria for the appraisal of art. As such, he was never understood. Instead, although it meant forgoing financial security, he remained true to his ideal of beauty and interpretation of art. While he managed to achieve a degree of recognition abroad, he was never able to convert this into financial success.

Nico's death in 1930, at the young age of 36, from meningitis, marked the end of the secessionist period in Luxembourg. The work of Nico Klopp only achieved a breakthrough after World War II, with three retrospectives finally bringing posthumous understanding and respect.

The 18th century master sculptors, Nicholas Jacques and Jean Georges Scholtus, are well-known within Luxembourg for their beautiful baroque high altars found in many of the old churches in the Ardennes and Mullerthal areas of the country. The War Memorial, a modern sculpture, is the work of Claus Cito, the winner of an international competition in 1923 for the best sculpturing work.

## CULTURAL MONUMENTS AND ARCHITECTURE

In 1994, the World Heritage Committee of UNESCO (United Nations Education, Scientific, and Cultural Organization) placed the old town and fortifications of Luxembourg City on its list of world cultural monuments. Divided into three areas, the first takes in the ancient quarters, including the original rock the city was founded on. The second brings together the governmental quarter, the Palace, and the cathedrals, and the third the battlements and towers, which secured the city to the east from the 14th century onwards.

Over the centuries, Luxembourg has seen many architectural changes. Many farmhouses from the 16th and 17th centuries, recognizable by their Renaissance-style front doors with a coat of arms and the partly mullioned windows, still exist. The larger farms often had a large entrance gate to the courtyard. During the 18th century, equally impressive farmhouses were built. Typically these had symmetrical fronts with a white outside coating, window lintels in the shape of a segmental arch, and beautifully sculptured front doors made from oak with frames of stone.

By the 19th century, the most significant buildings were the manor houses, which retained symmetrical fronts and stone frames.

## *MODERN ARCHITECTURE*

Modern architecture presents a startlingly different concept, especially office building design, with many of the banking houses and European institution buildings breaking with the tradition that architecture must be functional. Some 31% of the city center is taken up by offices. In the last decade, however, much of the building growth has taken place outside the center, especially in the Kirchberg Plateau area.

The Court of Justice, a five-storied building, was inspired by Luxembourg architect, Francis Jamagne, and two others from Belgium. Their vision was to embody "the concept of progressive law in a concrete symbol." The building, erected on a raised base in the center of a tiled plaza, with terracing surrounded by native trees, is constructed from a type of steel in which corrosion stabilizes after two years. It leaves a pleasing bronze tint, which improves with age and doesn't require attention. Another local architect, Pierre Bohler, had a major hand in the design of the European Center, constructed to host large conferences.

## LUXEMBOURG: EUROPEAN CITY OF CULTURE

A decade after an ambitious cultural plan, the European Cities of Culture, was launched in 1985 through the auspices of the EU, Luxembourg City was chosen to be the European City of Culture 1995. This concept of cultural exchange is not a new one for Luxembourg. In the early 1920s, Aline Mayrisch and her husband, model industrialist philanthropists, welcomed many of the greatest artists, philosophers, and poets of Europe to their home for a dialogue of cultures.

For the organizers of the 1995 festival, the aim was more complex. On one level it was to get artists of all genres from many countries to present their creations in the Grand Duchy and stimulate artistic production. The other goal, a demonstration that culture can be an engine of change for positive social growth, reaches far beyond that of a simple cultural event.

By bringing together local artists with international stars, and by encompassing every field of artistic creation, the desire was to provoke dialogue and be catalysts for multicultural encounters. Luxembourg is ideally placed because of its geographical position and mixture of nationalities to prove that coexistence and exchange of different cultures do not lead to the dilution of a country's identity, but to its enrichment.

The festival, containing some 500 events, was designed to alternate guest appearances and local productions alongside world premier events. Main productions included a drama by the Chilean writer, Marco Antonio de la Parra, the world premier of the opera *Elektra* from Warsaw, concerts by the British Royal and the Israel Philharmonic Orchestras, exhibitions of over 250 works by French post-impressionists, as well as original works by Luxembourg composers, music performances, and encounters with writers, mime artists, and sculptors.

The new HypoBank is considered an architectural masterpiece because, inconspicuous at first, the building slowly reveals its true nature with its changing pattern of forms from cubic to cylindrical. An imposing bronze sculpture stands in the entranceway.

Yet another bank, with the entrance hall made completely of glass and a concave grid under a glass roof, is spectacular because of the clear lines, the play of light and shade, and the inclusion of the sky as if it were an integral part of the construction.

# LEISURE

LUXEMBOURGERS HAVE EARNED A REPUTATION for working hard and taking life seriously. Nonetheless, with an average working week of 39 hours, and at least four weeks holiday a year, they also have considerable leisure time.

In a 1994 Euro-survey about favorite leisure activities, the most popular Luxembourger answers were "sleeping" and "resting". However, this does not present an accurate picture of Luxembourgers. Though they may not be fanatical sports enthusiasts, they do involve themselves in active recreation whenever possible. Fitness and health awareness is a concept that is slowly becoming part of the average person's lifestyle. Still, it would be true to say that Luxembourgers do like to spend a lot of their free time at home.

## VACATIONS

For many Luxembourgers, vacations are more often spent abroad than at home. With no beaches or mountain resorts in Luxembourg, there is little opportunity for swimming, sunbathing, or skiing that can be found in some other parts of Europe.

Moreover, Luxembourg's climate does not really attract Luxembourgers to spend their precious time off in their own country. Warmth and sunshine in the Mediterranean beckon those who can afford it. Reasonably priced package holidays are easily available.

With the opening of the Tunnel, the great engineering feat under the English Channel, linking Europe to Great Britain, Luxembourgers are also increasingly interested to visit Great Britain.

*Above:* **Fishing can be more than just a pastime for some enthusiasts. Those who fancy their chances can take part in the international fishing competitions that are held from July through to October, mostly along the Moselle and Sûre Rivers.**

*Opposite:* **Despite its small population, Luxembourg has an astonishing 19 riding schools— testimony to the popularity of this recreational activity with Luxembourger girls.**

97

## NATIONAL SPORTS

Luxembourgers enjoy sports activities, although many prefer to watch rather than participate. There are 57 sports associations in the country, covering all disciplines. However, only a few of these sports are highly regarded and followed avidly by the fans.

Luxembourg's national sport is soccer, which is played at the international level at the European championships. Roby Langers is a skilled player and a popular figure in the world of soccer, and one of the few professional athletes native to Luxembourg. Unfortunately, mob violence and hooliganism have marred a number of the European championship games.

American football, on the other hand, has never really caught the imagination of Luxembourgers in the same way as soccer, although there is a national team that plays—the Luxembourg Lions. Basketball, with national leagues for women as well as men, is an increasingly popular game and participation in the European championships is taken seriously. Favorite players include the 6ft 8in (2.03 m) forward Roby Horsmans and the young Marc Schiltz. The coach, Doug Marty, is originally from California.

The third most popular sport, in terms of the number of spectators it attracts, is tennis. An indoor tennis tournament, the Luxembourg Open, takes place every year. Also growing in spectator attraction is ice hockey, as represented by the Luxembourg team called Tornado.

Besides these sports, there are also many other lesser sports in terms of supporters and

Tennis is one of the more popular sports in Luxembourg.

## OLYMPIC CHAMPIONS

Luxembourg's first Olympic gold medallist was Michael Theato, who won the marathon at the Olympic Games in Paris in 1900. As no Olympic committee existed in the Grand Duchy at the time, Theato had to register under the colors of a French club, and for a long time was considered to be French. He ran a tactically clever race by letting other competitors lead the event. Coming to the front only at the last six miles (10 km), and to the applause of 1,500 spectators, he won after 2 hours, 59 minutes, and 45 seconds. He injured himself in his last race, the Tour de Paris, in 1903, finishing in 17th place. This effectively ended his sporting career.

Joseph Alzin was the second Luxembourger to win an Olympic medal—a silver at the 1920 Games in Antwerp, Belgium for weightlifting. But it was Josy Barthel, winning gold in the 1,500 meters at Helsinki in 1952, who really won the hearts of the people. Against all odds, Barthel beat the favorite from the United States. In Barthel's words, "I crossed the finish as I had always imagined in my secret dreams: hands up and smiling." Josy Barthel went on to head the Luxembourg Athletics Federation and ultimately the Olympic and Sports Committee of Luxembourg. The main sports stadium in Luxembourg is named after him.

Skier Marc Girardelli, although born in Austria, is now a national of Luxembourg and has won the World Cup championship five times. He also carried off two silver medals in the giant slalom and super-G at the Winter Games of Albertville in 1992. In 1994, at the age of 30, he came seventh in the World Cup downhill championship.

*In 1995 the Olympic and Sports Committee of Luxembourg (C.O.S.L.) organized the 6th Games of the Small European States, under the patronage of the Grand Duke Jean. This unites the best sportsmen and women from European countries with a population of less than one million people—Andorra, Cyprus, Iceland, Liechtenstein, Luxembourg, Malta, Monaco, and San Marino. More than 1,000 athletes took part in the Games, competing in sports like athletics, basketball, cycling, swimming, judo, tennis, and volleyball.*

earning potential, but with more actual participation among Luxembourgers. One is table tennis, displayed by the skills of Daniel Wintersdorff and Peggy Regenwetter. Another is gymnastics, which is pursued by young people and adults up to championship level. International semi-marathons take place, usually in September, with the course winding along the vine-growing valley of the Moselle. The names of Jean-Pierre Ernzen and Nancy Kemp-Arendt, who is also a triathlete, are becoming well-known on the marathon circuit, as is Laurent Kemp in track and field events.

Swimming has not always been a sport excelled in by Luxembourgers, but this is changing with the advent of Yves Clausse. Equestrian events, like show-jumping and dressage, are also held annually at Cup level.

## RECREATION

With a dense network of marked walking paths, and special pedestrian circuits through the forests in the Ardennes, hiking is a popular activity amongst Luxembourgers. Totally leaving civilization behind is difficult to achieve, though, as one is never more than five miles (8 km) away from a village or farm.

For those who wish to extend hiking excursions into more than day trips, campgrounds are everywhere, and numerous youth hostels are well-situated close to campsites should the weather turn rainy. Even in the southern industrial part of the country, walking trails, some up to 73 miles (117 km) long, can be found.

Bicycling is a national pastime. It is not uncommon to see elderly people cycling. In the summer the weather is especially conducive for cycling through the not-too-difficult Luxembourg terrain. There are traffic-free bicycle trails over much of Luxembourg along the scenic main rivers.

Other pursuits, such as kayaking and canoeing, are becoming increasingly popular because of the country's many rivers. Luxembourg also has a number of golf courses. Rock-climbing, fishing, and hunting are all popular activities. A particular favorite, especially with young girls, is horseback riding.

## ENTERTAINMENT

European statisticians, trying to measure the proportion of income spent on entertainment in the member states, put the Grand Duchy at the bottom of their "EU fun index" in 1994. However, the low figure of 4.3% is not a true reflection of what Luxembourg has to offer.

Nightlife is excellent in Luxembourg, as there is a good mix of bars, restaurants, and clubs run by Luxembourgers as well as other nationalities. One can play darts in British pubs or sing in Japanese Karaoke bars. In these well-patronized places, mainstream live music from piano to folk to blues and rock can be found.

International rock and roll groups like the Rolling Stones, for example, perform here regularly. The capital setting is ideal to attract crowds of young people from neighboring parts of Germany, France, and Belgium because they are within easy reach.

Other ways Luxembourgers spend their time include watching television, movies, and visiting cafés, the equivalent of bars. Movies are released early in Luxembourg and are dubbed in French and German. Going to the municipal theater can be difficult though as most of the seats are sold out to season ticket holders.

**Young Luxembourgers enjoy a day out at the fair.**

**101**

# FESTIVALS

LUXEMBOURGERS LOVE TO CELEBRATE festivals and seem to have a festival for almost every occasion, even though the origins of some are so ancient most people have forgotten them.

Many festivals are connected with religious observances, but there are also many that reflect the Luxembourgers' culture and lifestyle.

## NATIONAL DAY

Luxembourgers celebrate the birthday of their Grand Duke on 23 June, although his actual birthday is in January. This holiday is also considered the country's National Day. Many Luxembourgers use this day for shopping trips across the border, where it is not a public holiday. All over the country, National Day is an occasion for a happy and festive celebration, with traditional and patriotic processions, religious services, concerts, and public dances.

Festivities start on the day before with members of the Grand Ducal family being welcomed in various towns and villages of the country. Later, in the evening, Luxembourg City is flooded with lights and a torchlight parade is held in the capital, followed by a large firework display. On the day itself, crowds gather to watch the military parade. This is followed by a religious service in the presence of the Grand Ducal family.

Afterwards all the family members make a public appearance on the balcony of the Palace. On successive evenings for the rest of the week, various receptions of diplomatic corps and Luxembourg notables are held in the Palace.

*Above:* **A crowned car draws the crowds at a night carnival parade.**

*Opposite:* **Fireworks light up the night sky over the Adolphe Bridge in Luxembourg City.**

Every year, crowds throng the capital city's streets for the Easter market of *Emaischen*.

## *EASTER*

On Easter Sunday children traditionally look for Easter eggs hidden by the "Easter Rabbit," although this is more difficult to carry out in a modern apartment than in the countryside where the custom originated. Once the eggs have all been found, there is a friendly competition between the children who knock their eggs against each other's eggs. Those whose shells break lose. Typically the four-day Easter holiday is reserved for the first real spring outing of the year. By this time, the weather would have improved and there is a two-week school vacation.

Easter Monday is a public holiday. In the capital's old town a traditional colorful market called *Emaischen* ("E-MAY-schen") takes place. Once, pottery and other household wares were displayed, but now it is mainly popular arts and crafts. There are also games for children, folk dances, and singing.

## NATIONAL HOLIDAYS IN LUXEMBOURG

| | |
|---|---|
| January 1 | New Year's Day |
| March/April | Easter |
| May 5/6 | Labor Day |
| varies | Ascension Day |
| varies | Whitsun |
| June 23 | National Day |
| Nov 1 | All Saints' Day |
| Dec 25 | Christmas |
| Dec 26 | Boxing Day |

## CHRISTMAS

Another two-week school vacation occurs around Christmas and many people go abroad to escape the cold weather. Stores everywhere during this season are aglitter with decorations, while in the streets everything is festooned and illuminated for the season of goodwill.

The Christmas festivities begin on the feast of *Niklosdag* ("NICK-los-dag"), St. Nicholas' Day, on December 6. Each year *Kleeschen* ("CLE-schen"), or Father Christmas, dressed in a bishop's garb and holding a miter, comes down from the skies to reward the children who have been good throughout the year.

He and the *Housecker* ("HUSE-eck-er"), a swarthy companion dressed in a hooded monk's sack and carrying long sticks with which to chastise naughty children, are welcomed in the various towns and villages. After a procession, St. Nicholas gives sweets to the children who up till about the age of eight, get their presents on this day.

Christmas is also a time for feasting, with plenty of log cakes for everyone.

Christmas Eve is the family day when children, parents, and grandparents gather around the Christmas tree, exchange presents, listen to carols, and have a sumptuous meal. Unlike in the United States, turkey is not a must here. Instead, many Luxembourgers prefer ham or pork. Christmas Eve is also one of the few days of the year when children are allowed to stay up later. Frequently the whole family attends Midnight Mass celebrating the birth of Christ. Many workers are granted unofficial leave from their jobs for the afternoon.

On Christmas Day, lunch, interrupted only by a television speech from the Grand Duke, is usually hosted by an older member of the family, such as a grandparent. The day can be somewhat soporific after all the eating of the preceding evening. St. Stephen's Day, *Stiefesdag* ("SHTEEF-fes-dag"), is the day after Christmas and is another holiday with more feasting.

## NEW YEAR

New Year's Eve, marking the end of the year, is celebrated with friends, rather than family. This can be either at home or in a restaurant. Many of those who eat at home, watching television, will venture out to one of the many "Sylvester" balls. So named because December 31 is St. Sylvester's Day, these are dances in honor of a new year ahead. At midnight everyone wishes each other a Happy New Year and people kiss, pop champagne corks, and light fireworks.

The capital city, in particular, gets caught up in the party mood. The atmosphere is one of carnival-style decorations and firecrackers, which adds up to a noisy and colorful celebration.

New Year's Day, a public holiday devoted to sleeping late and visiting the family, can appear dull to many Luxembourgers compared to the previous night's excitement. The Prime Minister traditionally makes a speech on television as a start to the New Year.

## CUSTOMS AND RITUALS

January 6 in the Christian calendar is the feast of Epiphany, when the three Kings came to visit the baby Jesus after his birth. On this day a special almond cake is made, containing a miniature figure of a King. In the days of old, the cake contained a simple, plain bean.

The person who managed to collect the piece with the King's figure—usually one of the children, of course—is appointed King for the day, or even a week. This lucky person enjoys certain privileges, such as the right to decide on the meals for the next few days.

*Although New Year's Eve is not a public holiday, employees are usually allowed to go home at noon to prepare for the big night.*

**A reenactment display of the birth of Jesus.**

**Luxembourgers enjoy taking part in night processions.**

*In the town of Vianden in November,* Miertchen *("MI-air-shen"), St. Martin's Fire, takes place. This is an ancient custom celebrates the end of the harvest and the payment of the levy to the feudal lord.*

*Bretzelsonndeg* ("BRET-zel-son-deg") in March is Pretzel Sunday. According to tradition, the sequence of which is the subject of some debate, a young man offers his girlfriend a present on Valentine's Day to signal his love. If she responds favorably by offering him a pretzel on Pretzel Sunday, he then confirms his intentions by offering her Easter eggs at Easter. Thus the day has become one dedicated to lovers who give pretzels to each other and is celebrated by displays of folk art.

During the three days leading up to Easter Sunday, a tradition called *Klibberegoen* ("KLI-bare-gurn"), or Rattles Round, takes place. According to legend, all the bells in the parish churches fall silent at this time and fly away to Rome for confession. To replace the church bells, local boys have to do the rounds of the streets, reminding people of mass, by using rattles with their characteristic dry sound.

After the return of the bells, the boys call on each house to collect their brightly colored Easter eggs. Alongside this Rattles Round, other children walk behind a dog rose bush covered in paper flowers and multicolored ribbons, called the *Jaudes* ("U-des," Judas), as in Judas who betrayed Jesus Christ. After the last Rattles Round has taken place, *Jaudes* is burned.

*Schueberfouer* ("SHOO-bare-foor") is celebrated on September 3. This former shepherds' market, founded in 1340 by Count John the Blind, has become the capital's giant funfair. Sheep decorated with colorful ribbons are led by shepherds, dressed in folk costume, through the inner quarters of the city. They are accompanied by a band playing a lively tune—the *Hammelsmarsch* ("HAMM-els-marsh"), the sheep's march.

## PAGAN PRACTICES

The second of February is *Lichtmess* ("LICH-ter-mess"). This is an end of winter ritual devoted to the "new light," or the end of the short, dark days of winter. Children go from house to house carrying tapers and lamps and singing traditional songs. Their reward is sweets, but in the olden times, it was more basic necessities, such as lard and peas!

On the 25th day of the same month, *Burghrennen* ("BORG-bren-en"), or castle burning, takes place. This is another end of winter custom, where groups of children, usually boy scouts and girl-guides, gather on nearby hills and set fire to giant crosses made of wood and straw. The idea is to expel the darkness of winter. This pagan ritual of burning crosses forms a chain all over the hills, and is accompanied by barbecues and hot red wine.

## *FAIRS AND FETES*

Luxembourg has a long history of fetes and fairs, which are always accompanied by colorful processions, musical bands, flowers, and parades. Every village has its own *Kiirmes* ("KEER-mes"), or village fair, on the anniversary of its local saint.

Carnival week is February 20 to 25 and coincides with a one-week school holiday. It is a week of fun before the somber season of Lent in the Catholic calendar begins. During this time, the "Carnival Prince" reigns supreme.

Traditional dances such as this provide Luxembourgers with a link to their cultural heritage.

In the afternoons there are carnival processions with floats, sessions of public readings, and theme pageants. Costume balls are held in the evenings with music groups also in disguise. On Ash Wednesday, February 21, which is the beginning of Lent, young people in the Moselle valley carry a huge straw doll around the streets. On the bridge they set fire to it and throw it into the river to herald the end of the joyful Moselle carnival.

The first week in May is the beginning of spring fetes and members of local societies enter the woods to cut the first green branches. These are fashioned into a four-foot (1.2 m) diameter crown, a symbol of the reawakening of nature, called *Meekrantz* ("MEER-kruntz"), which is then carried in processions led by bands in most villages. This is also the time of another public holiday, Labor Day, recognized by trade union rallies with speeches.

*Whitsun Monday, the last Monday in May, is marked by the broom blossoms fair, Genzefest ("GEN-ze-fest"), with pageants and flower chariots in the north of the country.*

A religious procession makes its way through the streets of Luxembourg City.

## RELIGIOUS FESTIVALS

The two-week religious festival of Octave from May 7 to 21 is centered on a pilgrimage, in honor of Our Lady of Luxembourg, to the Cathedral Notre Dame. Delegations from all the parishes in the counties attend this pilgrimage. Many have to leave in the night to get there on time, usually traveling on foot as part of the pilgrimage. On the square in front of the cathedral, a fairground atmosphere prevails, with food stands serving fried fish, candy stalls, and religious souvenirs. May 21 marks the closing ceremony of the Octave. Stately solemn processions are held with the Royal Family and various Catholic dignitaries from abroad taking part in this grand ceremonial occasion.

Since 1628, Catholics of the Grand Duchy and neighboring regions have come to venerate the "Comforter of the Afflicted." The cult of Our Lady remains important to Luxembourg, even in an increasingly lay society, as it also symbolizes national identity and independence. On

Ascension Day, May 16, another pilgrimage to the nearby shrine of Our Lady of Fatima takes place.

Whitsun holiday is the name given to the religious time of Pentecost and usually falls on the last weekend of May. At the town of Kaundorf, a procession across fields and forests to St. Pirmin's fountain is held. According to legend, St. Pirmin was cured of an eye disease at the beginning of the 8th century after washing his eyes in the waters of the spring. Healing virtues are still attached to these waters.

Whit Tuesday, although not an official holiday, sees the Echternach dancing procession in honor of St. Willibrord, who died in Echternach in 739. This unique religious tradition, originally intended as a protection against epilepsy, attracts thousands of pilgrims and spectators.

The Echternach dancing procession has become one of Luxembourg's biggest tourist attractions.

The dancers, in rows eight or nine wide, take two steps forward and one step back and are joined by a line of white handkerchiefs. Each group of jumpers is accompanied by fiddlers who play a haunting polka. This colorful procession winds its way through the old cobbled streets of Echternach before returning to the Basilica church.

Assumption Day, *Leiffraweschdag* ("LEE-fraul-sch-dag"), is cause for another main celebration in honor of Our Lady. Various herbs, corn, and other plants are gathered in bouquets, which are presented as offerings at various country chapels.

All Saints' Day, which falls on November 1, is a time for religious ceremonies in churchyards. The tombs are blessed and the memory of the dead revered. Family members meet at the graves of their relatives and the ceremonies are usually followed by gatherings at home or in a restaurant.

# FOOD

THE TASTES OF LUXEMBOURGERS, who are very fond of their food, range widely, with all the international cuisines represented in the capital. Generally, they like to combine French quality with German quantity.

## *TRADITIONAL FARE*

There are a number of dishes that are considered traditional rural cooking. Such meals are simple and homely in style, but nourishing and wholesome in content.

Typically a first course would be *Bounnenschlupp* ("BORN-nen-shlup"), a bean soup. Many types of beans can be used, but the most common is the broad bean. Also taken as an entrée are *Quenelles* ("keh-nells"), small oval-shaped dumplings. Its base can be ground meat or fish. Fish *Quenelles* are prepared with a rich cream sauce, while the meat versions have an equally rich brown sauce.

*Opposite:* **A vegetable vendor sets up an open-air stall in the center of Luxembourg City.**

*Below:* **Snack stalls, such as this at the Place D'Armes in Luxembourg City, are popular with both locals and tourists.**

After the soup or entrée, the main course follows. Sometimes the *Quenelles*, usually meat ones, are eaten as a main meal. Such a dish would be accompanied by sauerkraut and boiled potatoes. One very popular dish is *Judd mat Gaardebounnen* ("udd mat gard-DA-born-nen"), smoked neck of pork in a delicious herb sauce accompanied by broad beans and boiled potatoes. Another is *Treipen* ("TRAY-pen"), black pudding or small hot sausages, with horse-radish, mashed potatoes, and sauerkraut.

*Feierstengszalot* ("fire-STENG-za-lot"), a salad composed of sliced cold beef with boiled egg and onions in an oil and vinegar dressing, is a quick and tasty meal. A more acquired taste is *Kuddelfleck* ("KU-del-fleck"), boiled tripe, which comes from the stomach lining of cattle and is classified as offal. Resembling a honeycomb in appearance, tripe is rich in gelatine, calcium, and iron, with a very low caloric value. Tripe usually requires prolonged cooking, but it is often sold partly cooked and blanched. *Gras Double Provencale* ("grah doobl proh-vahn-SAL"), tripe cooked with onion, garlic, and white wine, is an economical and tasty dish.

Delicious Ardennes ham, or *Fierkelsjhelle* ("fear-KUL-hel-la"), roasted suckling pig covered in an aspic sauce, is reserved for more special occasions. It is usually followed by cheese, particularly *Kachkéis* ("KARCH-kays"), typical soft and sticky boiled cheese. Dessert is not normally served with everyday meals, but can be expected to make an appearance at weekends, as would liqueur.

*Sauerkraut is a German food , but very popular in Luxembourg. Originally devised as a way of keeping vitamin-packed white cabbage through the winter, it is mixed with salt and wine and left to ferment.*

## *QUENELLES DE TRUITE* (TROUT *QUENELLES*)

*Quenelles de Truite* ("keh-nell de TRWEET") is often served as a garnish for any fish dish.

| | |
|---|---|
| 2 tablespoons butter | 1 egg, slightly beaten |
| $1/2$ cup flour | $1/4$ teaspoon salt |
| $1/4$ cup heavy cream | $1/4$ teaspoon white pepper |
| 6 oz (170 g) trout, filleted and ground | $1/8$ teaspoon cayenne |

Method:
1. Melt half of the butter and stir in the flour to make a smooth paste. Gradually add cream.
2. Cook, stirring constantly, for three minutes until a thick paste forms.
3. Remove from heat and stir in the trout and remaining ingredients. Beat the mixture well and spoon into a bowl, cover, and chill for 30 minutes.
4. With the remaining butter, grease a large saucepan. Fill it half-full with water and bring to a boil.
5. Dip a teaspoon in cold water and scoop out some of the fish mixture. Using another spoon do the same again and press the two halves together.
6. Drop the shapes into the hot water and cook 8 to 10 *Quenelles* at a time. Cook for 10 to 15 minutes or until they are puffed up.
7. Using a slotted spoon, remove the *Quenelles* and place on a plate to drain. Keep warm until ready to serve.

Two Luxembourgers enjoy a meal at a sidewalk restaurant. As in most of Europe, Luxembourgers prefer their coffee very strong and black. For those with a sweet tooth, sugar is added.

## *EATING HABITS*

A variety of vegetables, either grown locally or imported from Belgium and the Netherlands, are eaten in Luxembourg. An increasing quantity and diversity of exotic fruit from the Far East and South America can also be bought in the markets. Meat, fish, and game are popular, prepared either in a traditional manner, or in a slightly more sophisticated style, when inspired by French cuisine.

Most working Luxembourgers take little, if any, food for breakfast, unless they are on holiday and have that extra time. Coffee, rarely tea, bread, and jam is what is usually eaten—a continental breakfast. Lunch was once the main meal, but because of working habits and short lunch breaks, the main meal is now taken in the evening between 6.30 and 7.30. One course is served, with soup as starters, and cheese reserved for formal occasions or Sunday meals.

Many workers in the service industries in the capital take their lunch in restaurants, all of which offer varying courses or menus of the day. Great efforts are being made to develop cafeterias in schools, which at present close between 12 and 2.

The traditional family outing is Sunday lunch, or increasingly, brunch. The meal usually takes the form of a buffet, which includes hot dishes. Meals accompanying special occasions, such as anniversaries, success at exams, religious events like Baptism, First Communion, and Confirmation, which used to be eaten at home, are now more frequently transferred to restaurants.

*In early October, in Vianden, a large walnut market is set up, with sales of fresh walnuts, walnut cake, walnut candy, and walnut liqueur from roadside stalls.*

## SPECIALTIES

Confectionery and assorted chocolates are a special feature in the Luxembourg pastry shops. A true specialty is *Quetschentaart* ("ketch-en-TART"), which is a plum tart made from small plums and the liqueur *Quetsch*.

The best chocolates are those made by hand, using the best chocolate, fresh cream, and butter, with no added preservatives. Some contain fruit and nuts, while others contain liqueur. Somewhat expensive, they are intended for the true connoisseur. Freshly made the day before they are sold, they will not last more than three days, but the difference in taste between these and factory-made ones makes this disadvantage worthwhile.

**Mushrooms galore! This display, which comes in all shapes and sizes, is a feast for the eyes.**

During the carnival season, a special pastry called *Les Pensees Broulilles* ("les PON-ci BREW-li-les"), literally "puzzled thoughts," is available in abundance. These are delicious fried knots of dough and are a favorite with young and old alike.

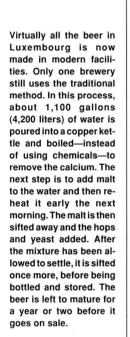

Virtually all the beer in Luxembourg is now made in modern facilities. Only one brewery still uses the traditional method. In this process, about 1,100 gallons (4,200 liters) of water is poured into a copper kettle and boiled—instead of using chemicals—to remove the calcium. The next step is to add malt to the water and then reheat it early the next morning. The malt is then sifted away and the hops and yeast added. After the mixture has been allowed to settle, it is sifted once more, before being bottled and stored. The beer is left to mature for a year or two before it goes on sale.

*Opposite:* **One of Luxembourg's wine caves. The country also has a small, but growing reputation for its liqueurs. Quetsch, Mirabelle, Kirsch, and Prunelle liqueurs are all derived from fruit trees. The quality of these drinks is stamped with the mark of approval from the state in the same way as the wines, so quality is guaranteed.**

## *A NATION OF DRINKERS*

The range of beers and wines consumed in Luxembourg has dramatically increased and become truly international since the opening of European borders. Special supporting fraternities have even grown up around these two types of drinks. Per person, Luxembourg has the highest beer production in the world, but that also includes production for export.

Although brewing is a traditional industry in the Grand Duchy, beer is now produced in modern breweries. "Pure malt and hop" is the motto and Luxembourg beers, particularly the dark kind, are becoming increasingly popular abroad.

There is still a brewery at Bascharage in the south, where one can learn about the production processes and taste the various brews. The small family-owned brewery still uses traditional methods.

## WINES

Wines from the Moselle valley have gained a reputation as quality wines for everyday consumption. They are completely different in taste, though not in names, from their German Mosel counterparts. The former are less sweet and resemble those from France.

The "Cremant de Luxembourg" label was introduced in 1988 exclusively for sparkling wines, which are produced by the "method of Champagne." According to this method, the grapes are pressed and the juice allowed to ferment in huge metal vats.

The wine is mixed, sugar and yeast added, and then bottled and corked. The extra sugar and yeast cause a second fermentation in the bottle and makes the wine fizzy. Sediment is removed and then the bottle recorked. This method is time-consuming and expensive, but makes for a very popular export product.

The wine cellars, six in the Moselle valley, are open to visitors in the summer months and are popular spots to visit and do some wine-tasting. Some of the smaller caves have become regular meeting spots for the local older folk on Sunday mornings. In the summer it is also possible to travel the "wine river" on board a cruise ship, which plies the Moselle, calling in at the major towns along the way.

During the hunting season, the most common game includes pheasant, young boar, venison, and wild rabbit. The meat is often marinaded in red wine and then stewed. Recipes for game dishes are guarded zealously and only the hunters or their wives consider themselves qualified to prepare such meals!

## *SEASONAL FOODS*

From March through the end of September, fish such as trout, crawfish, pike, and other highly prized small fish from the Sûre, Moselle, and Our can be found in abundance. Pike is a freshwater game fish and is reputed to kill and eat its own kind. It can grow to as much as 70 lbs (31.5 kg). However, those eaten usually weigh from 3 to 6 lbs (1.3 to 2.7 kg). The flesh is firm and white, but tends to be dry and coarse, with many sharp bones. Though pike can be cooked in a variety of ways, it is most often used to make *Quenelles*.

Trout is from the same family as the salmon. It has a firm oily flesh and a sweet delicate flavor. Trout is a good source of protein and contains a small amount of almost every vitamin. The river trout found in Luxembourg has a skin varying in color from silvery-white to dark grey, and is speckled with red, brown, or black spots. The flesh is white in color. The trout is small, so one fish makes a portion for one person. Trout can be cooked either very simply by grilling, frying, or poaching, or used in *Quenelles*.

## EATING OUT

Luxembourg City has a great variety of restaurants, covering all tastes, nationalities, and prices. Restaurant food is popular as it offers an opportunity for dining out, meeting people, and enjoying food that is too difficult or time-consuming to prepare at home. French fries are frequently ordered, and a selection of vegetables is served with the dishes as an integral part of the meal.

One can choose from Italian or Spanish to Indian, Chinese, or Japanese. Pizzerias and Italian places are very popular with the young and are often crowded. Also trendy are Spanish restaurants with their *tapas* ("TAH-pahs"), a side-dish selection of snack food that accompanies beer, as well as Indian restaurants.

Within a few blocks, one can find both fast-food chains and also Michelin-star restaurants. To savor top-level French cuisine at lunch time, or on Friday and Saturday nights, booking a table is essential. Competition is fierce and patrons insist on both quality and quantity. Restaurants can become fashionable overnight and then disappear just as quickly if they can't keep up the quality or raise prices too much.

Many Luxembourgers prefer their own company and that of close friends, and like to keep their home life private. Rather than invite friends to visit, they prefer to go out in the evening and enjoy a meal at a restaurant.

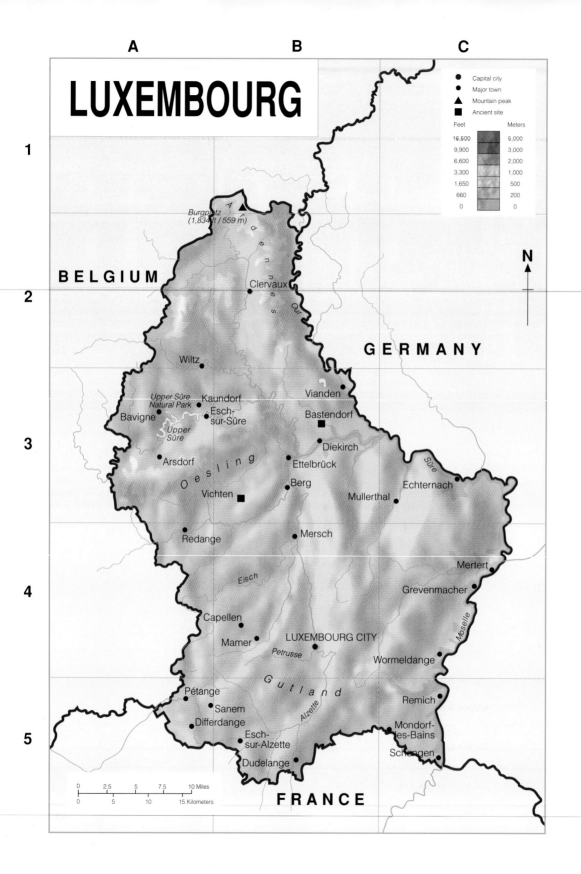

# LUXEMBOURG

**A**    **B**    **C**

1

| Legend | |
|---|---|
| ● | Capital city |
| ● | Major town |
| ▲ | Mountain peak |
| ■ | Ancient site |

| Feet | | Meters |
|---|---|---|
| 16,500 | | 5,000 |
| 9,900 | | 3,000 |
| 6,600 | | 2,000 |
| 3,300 | | 1,000 |
| 1,650 | | 500 |
| 660 | | 200 |
| 0 | | 0 |

*Burgplatz*
*(1,834 ft / 559 m)*

N

BELGIUM

2

Clervaux

GERMANY

Wiltz

Upper Sûre
Natural Park    Kaundorf
Esch-
sur-Sûre    Vianden
Bavigne    Bastendorf
Upper
Sûre    Diekirch
3    Arsdorf    *Oesling*    Ettelbrück    *Sûre*
Berg    Echternach
Vichten    Mullerthal

Redange    Mersch

*Eisch*    Mertert

4    Grevenmacher

Capellen    *Moselle*

Mamer    LUXEMBOURG CITY
*Petrusse*    Wormeldange

*Gutland*

Pétange    Remich
Sanem    *Alzette*
Differdange    Mondorf-
les-Bains
Esch-
5    sur-Alzette    Schengen

Dudelange

| | | | | 10 Miles |
|---|---|---|---|---|
| 0 | 2.5 | 5 | 7.5 | |
| 0 | | 5 | 10 | 15 Kilometers |

FRANCE

Alzette, B5
Ardennes, B2
Arsdorf, A3

Bastendorf, B3
Bavigne, A3
Belgium, A2
Berg, B3
Burgplatz, B1

Capellen, B4
Clervaux, B2

Diekirch, B3
Differdange, A5
Dudelange, B5

Echternach, C3
Eisch, B4
Esch-sur-Alzette, B5
Esch-sur-Sûre, A3
Ettelbrück, B3

France, B5

Germany, C2
Grevenmacher, C4
Gutland, B5

Kaundorf, A3

Luxembourg City, B4

Mamer, B4
Mersch, B4
Mertert, C4
Mondorf-les-Bains, C5
Moselle, C4
Mullerthal, C3

Oesling, A3–B3
Our, B2

Pétange, A5
Petrusse, B4

Redange, A4
Remich, C5

Sanem, A5
Schengen, C5

Sûre, C3

Upper Sûre Natural Park,
  A3
Upper Sûre, A3

Vianden, B3
Vichten, B3

Wiltz, A2
Wormeldange, C4

# QUICK NOTES

**AREA**
998 square miles (2,586 square kilometers)

**POPULATION**
406,600 (1995 estimate)

**CAPITAL**
Luxembourg City

**OFFICIAL NAME**
Grand Duchy of Luxembourg

**MAJOR LANGUAGES**
Letzenburgish (national language)
German
French

**HIGHEST POINT**
Burgplatz (1,834 feet / 559 meters)

**MAJOR LAKE**
Upper Sûre

**MAJOR RELIGION**
Roman Catholicism

**MAJOR RIVERS**
Moselle, Our, Sûre, Alzette, Petrusse

**NATIONAL FLOWER**
The rose

**COAT OF ARMS**
Cross bars of silver and blue, and a red lion
rampant crowned with gold.

**MAJOR CITIES**
Differdange, Dudelange, Sanem, Esch-sur-
Alzette, Echternach

**NATIONAL FLAG**
Three horizontal bands of red, white, and blue

**CURRENCY**
Luxembourg Franc
1 franc = 100 centimes
US$1 = 31.3 franc

**MAIN EXPORTS**
Steel, wine, farm produce, and manufactured
goods

**MAJOR IMPORTS**
Machinery, electrical equipment, and fuel

**HEAD OF STATE**
Grand Duke Jean

**MAJOR RULERS AND POLITICAL LEADERS**
Siegfried, Count (963–998)
Ermesinde, Countess (1226–1247)
John the Blind, Count (1310–1346)
Charlotte, Grand Duchess (1919–1964)
Jean-Claude Juncker, prime minister since 1995

**SOME IMPORTANT ARTISTS**
Pierre Redoute, Nico Klopp, Jos Sunnen,
    Joseph Kutter

**ANNIVERSARIES**
National Day (June 23)

# GLOSSARY

**Bounnenschlupp** ("BORN-nen-shlup")
Bean soup, most commonly broad bean, to start off a meal.

**Bretzelsonndeg** ("BRET-zel-son-deg")
Pretzel Sunday.

**Burgbrennen** ("BORG-bren-en")
Castle burning, an end of winter custom performed in February.

**Emaischen** ("E-MAY-schen")
Traditional market held on Easter Monday in Luxembourg City.

**Fierkelsjhelle** ("fear-KUL-hel-la")
Roasted suckling pig covered in an aspic sauce.

**Gras Double Provencale** ("grah doobl proh-vahn-SAL")
Tripe cooked with onion, garlic, and white wine—an economical Luxembourg favorite.

**Hammelsmarsch** ("HAMM-els-marsh")
The sheep's march, a lively tune played during the shepherds' market.

**Housecker** ("HUSE-eck-er")
Father Christmas' swarthy companion who carries a long stick to chastise naughty children.

**Jaudes** ("U-des")
A dog rose bush covered in paper flowers and multicolored ribbons, made for the Rattles Round.

**Judd mat Gaardebounnen** ("udd mat gard-DA-born-nen")
Smoked neck of pork in herb sauce, with broad beans and boiled potatoes.

**Kachkéis** ("KARCH-kays")
Soft and sticky boiled cheese.

**Kiirmes** ("KEER-mes")
Village fair held on the anniversary of the local saint.

**Kleeschen** ("CLE-schen")
Father Christmas.

**Klibberegoen** ("KLI-bare-gurn")
Rattles Round, where boys roam the streets, using rattles to remind people of Mass in the three days leading up to Easter Sunday.

**Kuddelfleck** ("KU-del-fleck")
Boiled tripe.

**Lichtmess** ("LICH-ter-mess")
End of winter ritual celebrated in February, when children carry tapers and lamps and sing traditional songs.

**Miertchen** ("MI-air-shen")
St. Martin's Fire, an ancient custom in Vianden to celebrate the end of the harvest with huge bonfires and a torchlight procession.

**Niklosdag** ("NICK-los-dag")
St. Nicholas' Day, which falls on December 6.

**Quenelles** ("keh-nells")
Small oval-shaped meat or fish dumplings, which can be both an entrée or a main course.

**Schueberfouer** ("SHOO-bare-foor")
Former shepherds' market, now a giant funfair in the capital.

**Stiefesdag** ("SHTEEF-fes-dag")
St. Stephen's Day, the day after Christmas.

# BIBLIOGRAPHY

Barzini, Luigi. *The Europeans.* New York: Simon and Schuster, 1983.

Cameron, Fiona. *We live in Belgium and Luxembourg.* Sussex, England: Wayland, 1986.

Corrick, James. *The Late Middle Ages.* San Diego: Lucent Books, 1995.

Lewis, Flora. *Europe.* New York: Simon and Schuster, 1987.

Needham, Ed. *The Countries of Benelux.* London: Watts Books, 1994.

Netherlands Foundation. *The Low Countries.* 1993–4.

Stevenson, Victor. *Evolution of Western Languages.* New York: Nostrad Reinhold, 1990.

# INDEX

Adolphe, Duke, 22
agriculture, 10, 37, 45–46, 57
All Saints' Day, 104, 111
Alzin, Joseph, 99
ARBED, 41
archaeology, 87–88
architecture, 93–95
Ardennes, 7, 8, 87, 89, 91, 92, 100
army, 35
Ascension Day, 104, 111
Assumption Day, 111
Augustus, Emperor, 19

Bank of Credit and Commerce International, 44
banking, 37–40, 43–44, 87
Barthel, Josy, 99
Bascharage, 118
Bastendorf, 87
Bavigne, 75
Beatles, 85
Bech, Joseph, 54–55
beer, 118
Belgium, 3, 7, 10, 11, 19, 21–22, 23, 25, 38, 43, 47, 71, 94, 99, 101, 116

Benedictine Abbey, 17, 70
Benelux countries, 7, 26
Benelux Customs Union, 25
birth rate, 49, 63, 73
Bock, 20
*Bounnenschlupp,* 113
*Bretzelsonndeg,* 108
Bulge, battle of, 24
*Burgbrennen,* 109
Burgundians (Dukes of Burgundy), 21

Calvinism, 71
Cape Verde islanders, 52–53
Carnot, General, 23
casemates, 23
castle ruins, 12, 46
cattle, 9, 45
Celts, 19, 42
Chamber of Deputies, 29, 30
Charlemagne, 19
Charles, Count, 20
Charlotte, Grand Duchess, 22–23, 25, 33
children, 52, 59, 60, 63, 78, 79, 87, 104–107, 108–109
Christmas, 24, 104, 105–106

Churchill, Sir Winston, 50
cinema (movies), 79, 89, 101
Cito, Claus, 92
Coat of Arms, 33
communes, 31
Congress of Vienna, 22
constitution, 29
construction industry, 38, 41
Council of Ministers, 30
Council of State, 30
Court of Auditors, 40
crime rate, 65

de Cuellar, Perez, 57
Denmark, 57
Differdange, 17
divorces, 73
Druids, 69
Ducal Palace, 29, 103
Dudelange, 17
*Dullemajik,* 90

Easter, 104
Echternach, 17, 69, 70, 75, 88, 111
Echternach dancing procession, 111

# INDEX

education, 29, 61, 62–63, 71, 77, 78–79
elections, 29, 30–31, 34–35
*Emaischen*, 104
energy, 47
England (Great Britain), 23, 27, 32, 65, 67, 97
Epiphany, 107
Ermesinde, Countess, 20, 21, 91
Esch-sur-Alzette, 16–17
Esch-sur-Sûre, 12, 75
Eurobond, 40, 43
European Center, 94
European Coal and Steel Community (ECSC), 26, 27, 55
European Commission, 27
European Court of Justice, 3, 27, 40, 94
European Economic Community (EEC), 26
European Investment Bank, 3, 40, 44
European Parliament, 27, 35, 40
European Union (EU), 3, 26–27, 34, 39, 47, 57, 67, 81, 87, 95

Federspiel, Pierre, 91
*Feierstengszalot*, 114
Festival of Immigration, 52–53
*Fierkelsjhelle*, 115
Flesch, Colette, 35
foreign workers, 38
forestry, 12, 45
France, 3, 7, 11, 19, 21, 26, 38, 45, 47, 55, 77, 101, 119
Franks, 19

*Genzefest*, 109
Germany, 3, 7, 11, 17, 19, 23, 24, 26, 38, 47, 55, 57, 77, 83, 101
Gibraltar, 23
Girardelli, Marc, 99

*Gras Double Provencale*, 114
Gutland, 9–10

Habsburgs, 21
Hamm military cemetery, 24
*Hammelsmarsch*, 108
health care, 64
Heiderscheidergrunt, 75
Henry V, Count, 21, 33
*Housecker*, 105
housing, 53, 57–59

immigrants, 49, 52–53, 79, 82
Italy, 26

Jacques, Nicholas, 92
Japan, 37, 49
*Jaudes*, 108
Jean, Grand-Duke, 25, 29, 32–33, 99
Jesuits, 71
Jewish community, 73
John the Blind, Count, 20, 75, 108
Josephine-Charlotte, Princess, 25, 32
*Judd mat Gaardebounnen*, 114
judicial power, 32
Julius Caesar, 19
Juncker, Jean-Claude, 30, 34

*Kachkéis*, 115
*Kleeschen*, 105
*Klibberegoen*, 108
Klopp, Nico, 91–92
*Kuddelfleck*, 114
Kutter, Joseph, 91

language
    English, 82, 85
    French, 77–79, 82–85, 101
    German, 77–79, 82–85, 101
    Luxembourgish (Letzenburgish), 77–85
    Portuguese, 79
*Les Pensees Broulilles*, 117

*Lichtmess*, 109
Lippmann, Gabriel, 55
literature, 80
log cake, 106
Low Countries, 7, 21, 69, 71, 88
Luther, Martin, 70
Lutheranism, 70
Luxembourg City, 7–8, 15–16, 20–21, 34–35, 58, 92–93, 95, 103, 105, 113, 121
Luxembourg Model, 39

Maastricht Treaty, 26
Mamer, 88
manufacturing, 37–39, 41
Margaret, Princess, 85
*Meekrantz*, 109
*Miertchen*, 108
mining, 10, 41–42
Mnemosyne, 88
Monnet, Jean, 27
Monetary Institute, 43
monetary union, 26–27
Moselle valley, 13, 45–46, 99, 119
Mullerthal, 92
music, 90, 95

Napoleon Bonaparte, 21–22, 91
National Art and History Museum, 87
National Day (Grand Duke's Birthday), 33, 103–104
national anthem, 33
Netherlands, 7, 19, 21–22, 25, 33, 57, 71, 116
New Year, 104, 107
*Niklosdag*, 105
North Atlantic Treaty Organization (NATO), 25, 34–35
Notre Dame, Cathedral, 73–75, 110
nuclear weapons, 34

# INDEX

Octave, 73, 110
Olympic and Sports Committee
    of Luxembourg (C.O.S.L.),
    99
Olympic Games, 91, 99
Organization for Economic
    Cooperation and
    Development (OECD), 25
Oesling, 8–9, 10, 12, 100
otter, 14

Patton, General George S., 23,
    24
Poland, 25
Polfer, Lydie, 34–35
police, 32, 65
political parties, 34–35
pollution, 66–67

Quenelles, 113–115, 120
Quetschentaart, 117

Radio Luxembourg, 84–85
radio, 33, 84–85
rainfall, 13
recycling, 66–67
Redoute, Pierre, 91
referendum, 29, 77
Resistance movement, 23, 25,
    53
rivers
    Alzette, 11, 15, 20
    Eisch, 11
    Moselle, 7, 10, 11, 92, 97,
        109, 119–120
    Our, 11, 47, 120
    Petrusse, 11, 15, 20
    Rhine, 7, 11, 19
    Sûre, 9, 11, 17, 88, 97, 120
Roman Empire, 19, 74

Sanem, 17
Santer, Jacques, 27
Scholtus, Jean Georges, 92

Schueberfouer, 108
Schuman, Robert, 26–27, 55
Seimetz, Frantz, 91
Siegfried, 20
sports
    basketball, 98–99
    cycling, 100
    horse riding, 97, 101
    soccer, 98
    swimming, 99
    tennis, 98–99
Spain, 21, 23, 71–72
St. Ignatius, 71
St. Mary's Cathedral, 69
St. Willibrord, 69, 70, 75, 88, 111
steel, 10, 17, 37, 41–42, 47
Steichen, Edward, 92
Stiefesdag, 106
Sunnen, Jos, 91

taxation laws, 37, 43–44
television, 84–85, 89, 101, 106–107
theater, 80, 89, 101
Theato, Michael, 99
tourism, 12, 37, 46–47, 60
trade fairs, 42
traditional crafts, 88
Treaty of London, 22–23
Treipen, 114
Truman, President, 24

unemployment, 37–38, 53, 61
United Nations Education,
    Scientific, and Cultural
    Organization (UNESCO), 85, 93
United Nations (UN), 25, 55, 57
United States, 49, 51, 64, 79–80, 99,
    106
Upper Sûre dam, 12, 47
Upper Sûre lake, 12
Upper Sûre Natural Park, 9, 12

Vianden, 9, 75, 108, 117
Vichten, 88

War Memorial, 92
Whit Tuesday, 17, 111
Whitsun Monday, 109
Wilhemina, Queen, 22
William I, King, 22
William II, King, 19
William III, King, 22
Wiltz, 89
wine, 10, 12, 45–47, 118–119
witchcraft, 72
women, 35, 59–60
World War I, 23
World War II, 7, 23–25, 32–33,
    53–55, 85, 92

Zeus, 88